The She CEO Survival Guide

The Ultimate Guide to Surviving and Thriving as a Female CEO

Nancy A Brown

The She CEO Survival Guide

Copyright 2023 © Nancy A Brown

CONTENTS

Dedication

To my two children, Anthony and Alyssa, and my loving husband Larry,

This book is dedicated to you. Your unwavering support, love, and encouragement have been the foundation of my success.

You have inspired me to pursue my dreams and achieve my goals, even during the most challenging times.

Your belief in me has been a constant source of motivation, and I am forever grateful for your love and support.

May this book serve as a reminder of the importance of perseverance, determination, and the power of a strong support system. I love you all more than words can express.

About the Author

Meet Nancy A Brown, the author of "The She CEO Survival Guide". With over 25 years of experience in business and entrepreneurship, Nancy has faced and overcome numerous challenges in her career. As the CEO of Virtual Gal Friday, a virtual assistant agency, and a business and life coach, she has helped countless women entrepreneurs achieve their goals and thrive in the business world.

In addition to her extensive experience in business, Nancy is also a devoted wife and mother of two children, Anthony and Alyssa. As a working mother, she understands the challenges of balancing work and family responsibilities, and she is passionate about helping other women achieve this balance as well.

Through her work as a business and life coach, Nancy has seen first-hand the unique obstacles and barriers that women face in leadership roles. She wrote "The She CEO Survival Guide" to provide practical strategies and inspiring stories of successful women in business who have overcome these challenges and achieved great success.

Nancy's mission is to empower and inspire women to achieve their goals and make a positive impact in their organizations and communities. She believes that by supporting each other and sharing our experiences, we can create a more inclusive and supportive business environment for women.

Foreword

As a business owner and advocate for women in leadership roles, I am thrilled to introduce The She CEO Survival Guide. This guide is a valuable resource for women who are looking to overcome the unique challenges they may face in their professional lives.

As a fellow female entrepreneur, I know firsthand the struggles and obstacles that come with leadership. Throughout my 25-plus years in business and as a mother raising two children, I have encountered numerous challenges and setbacks. But I have also experienced great success, and I firmly believe that with the right tools and mindset, anything is possible.

The She CEO Survival Guide is an essential tool for any woman in business who wants to overcome obstacles and achieve success.

I am confident that The She CEO Survival Guide will be an invaluable resource for women in business. Its practical advice, inspiring stories, and actionable strategies can help you overcome obstacles, achieve success, and make a positive impact in your organization and beyond.

I encourage you to dive into this guide and explore the strategies and insights it offers. With determination, perseverance, and the right mindset, anything is possible.

THE SHE CEO SURVIVAL GUIDE

Nancy A Brown

CHAPTER 1

Introduction

I am thrilled to welcome you to "The She CEO Survival Guide"!

As a businesswoman with over 25 years of experience, I have faced unique challenges and obstacles in the business world. However, I have also learned valuable lessons and developed strategies for success that I am excited to share with you in this guide.

One of the challenges I faced was balancing my work and personal responsibilities while raising my children. I know firsthand how challenging it can be to manage both aspects of life, but I also believe that it's possible to find a balance that works for you. With the right mindset and support system, you can achieve your personal and professional goals.

Throughout this guide, we'll cover a range of topics that are relevant to women in business, from developing leadership skills and emotional intelligence, to accessing capital and funding, and building a strong personal and professional network.

We'll also explore strategies for overcoming self-doubt and imposter syndrome, managing difficult conversations and conflicts in the workplace, and staying up-to-date with industry trends and innovations.

I am excited to share inspiring stories of successful women in business who have overcome obstacles and achieved great things.

Their experiences demonstrate that with the right strategies, hard work, and determination, anything is possible.

My goal with this guide is to empower and inspire you to overcome challenges and achieve success in your own business journey. I believe that by supporting each other and sharing our experiences, we can create a more inclusive and supportive business environment for women.

So, whether you're just starting out in your entrepreneurial journey or looking to take your business to the next level, I hope that this guide will be a valuable resource for you. Let's work together to achieve our goals and make a positive impact in the business world.

Sincerely,

Definition of "She CEO"

As a woman who has navigated the business world for many years, I have witnessed firsthand the challenges that come with being a female chief executive officer. That's why I wrote this book, to provide guidance and support for women like me who aspire to become She CEOs.

The term "She CEO" refers to a woman who has risen to a position of leadership in the business world, whether she is leading a startup, a small business, or a large corporation. Despite the progress we've made towards gender equality, there are still unique challenges that women face in the business world, and I believe it's important to address these challenges and provide strategies for overcoming them.

A "She CEO" is a female chief executive officer who leads a company, whether it's a startup, small business, or large corporation. As the term implies, a She CEO is a woman who has broken through gender barriers and risen to a position of leadership in the business world.

Some examples of successful She CEOs include:

- Mary Barra, CEO of General Motors
- Ginni Rometty, former CEO of IBM
- Whitney Wolfe Herd, founder and CEO of Bumble
- Sara Blakely, founder and CEO of Spanx
- Anne Wojcicki, co-founder and CEO of 23andMe
- Reshma Saujani, founder and CEO of Girls Who Code

These women have demonstrated exceptional leadership skills and have succeeded in industries that have historically been male-dominated. They serve as role models for aspiring She CEOs and illustrate the potential for women to excel in leadership positions.

The term "She CEO" also highlights the unique challenges that women in leadership positions may face, such as gender bias and discrimination. By acknowledging these challenges and promoting the success of She CEOs, we can work towards greater gender equality in the business world.

In this book, we will provide strategies, insights, and inspiration for She CEOs who are looking to overcome challenges and achieve success in their businesses. We will cover a range of topics, including building a strong network, developing leadership skills, embracing innovation, and managing change. We hope that this book will serve as a valuable resource for She CEOs at all stages of their careers.

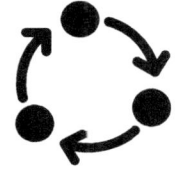

CHAPTER 2

The Challenges Women Face in Business

"I had to make my own living and my own opportunity! But I made it! Don't sit down and wait for the opportunities to come. Get up and make them." Madam C.J. Walker, the first female self-made millionaire in America

As a female CEO, I've come to realize that despite the progress towards gender equality in the business world, women still face unique challenges that can hinder our success. Believe me, I've been there myself, and I've seen many other women struggle with these issues too. These challenges can be subtle biases in the workplace or larger societal barriers that make it hard for women to access resources and opportunities. But here's the good news: in this chapter, we'll tackle some of the most common challenges that we face as women in business, such as gender bias, imposter syndrome, work-family balance, networking, and access to funding. By understanding these obstacles and developing strategies to overcome them, we can unleash our full potential and thrive in the business world.

Gender Bias in the Workplace & in the Marketplace

Let's talk about something that's unfortunately all too common in the world of business: gender bias. It's a sad reality that women still face discrimination and stereotypes when trying to make it in their careers or start their own businesses. From being talked over in meetings to facing unequal pay, these obstacles can make it feel like an uphill battle for women entrepreneurs.

But fear not, She CEOs! In this section of the Survival Guide, we'll take a closer look at the different ways that gender bias can rear its ugly head in the workplace and in the marketplace. We'll explore the research behind it, share real-life stories from successful women who have faced it head-on, and give you practical tips and strategies for combating bias and standing up for yourself and your business.

Remember, you are strong, capable, and deserving of success. And with the right tools and mindset, you can overcome the challenges of gender bias and achieve your dreams as a woman in business.

As you read through the following list, you'll see how gender bias can manifest itself in various ways in the workplace and in the marketplace, affecting women's opportunities for growth and success.

Pay inequity: Women are often paid less than their male counterparts, even when they have the same qualifications and experience.

According to the American Association of University Women (AAUW) report "The Simple Truth About the Gender Pay Gap," women in the United States are paid just 82 cents for every dollar earned by men. The report finds that the gender pay gap is present across all demographics, but it is particularly wide for women of color. For example, Black women are paid only 63 cents, Native American women are paid only 60 cents, and Latina women are paid only 55 cents for every dollar paid to white, non-Hispanic men. The report also notes that the pay gap widens over the course of a woman's career, with women earning less than men at every education level and in nearly every occupation. The AAUW report highlights the need for policy changes, including stronger equal pay laws and better workplace practices, to address the gender pay gap.

Lack of Opportunities: Women may face obstacles in accessing career advancement opportunities or leadership positions, despite having the necessary skills and qualifications.

The study by Moss-Racusin et al. (2012) found that science faculty members in the United States rated male job applicants as more competent and hireable than female applicants with identical qualifications. The researchers concluded that these biases were likely unconscious and unintentional, and they had a negative impact on the hiring and promotion of women in science. This study provides evidence of the subtle, yet pervasive nature of gender bias in the workplace, and highlights the need for greater awareness and action to combat it.

Stereotyping and Bias: Women may be stereotyped and discriminated against based on gender, race, age, or other factors, affecting their credibility, authority, and ability to make decisions.

Heilman and Okimoto's study (2007) suggests that when women are successful in tasks that are traditionally associated with men, they are often perceived as less likable, less competent, and less desirable as a coworker or a potential hire. This is due to what the authors call the "implied communality deficit," which means that women are perceived as less communal or less oriented towards others than men, especially in stereotypically masculine domains. As a result, women may be penalized for success in male-typed jobs or activities and may face a "double-bind" between being perceived as competent but unlikable or communal but incompetent. This study highlights the pervasive nature of gender bias and its impact on women's career advancement and success.

Microaggressions: Women may face subtle, everyday forms of discrimination, such as being interrupted or talked over in meetings, or having their ideas dismissed or ignored.

According to the "Women in the Workplace 2020" report by Lean In, microaggressions are a common form of bias that women face in the workplace. Microaggressions are subtle and often unintentional behaviors or comments that can convey negative messages or assumptions about a person's gender, race, or other identities.

For example, a microaggression towards a woman in the workplace might be assuming that she is responsible for taking notes in a meeting because of her gender, or interrupting her more frequently than male colleagues. The report notes that while these behaviors may seem small, they can accumulate over time and create a toxic workplace culture that undermines women's confidence and performance.

Access To Funding and Resources: Women may face challenges in securing funding or resources for their businesses, due to bias or discrimination in the financial industry.

There is a significant body of research that focuses on the challenges women face in accessing funding and resources for their businesses, due to various forms of gender bias and discrimination in the financial industry.

For example, a study by the National Women's Business Council (NWBC) found that women-owned businesses receive only 4.4% of total small business lending despite representing 42% of all U.S. businesses. The report suggests that unconscious bias and gender stereotypes among lenders, as well as the lack of women in positions of power in the financial industry, may contribute to this disparity.

Another study by researchers at Harvard Business School found that investors, both male and female, were more likely to invest in companies with pitches that used language associated with masculine stereotypes, such as "dominate" and "crush." This can put women entrepreneurs at a disadvantage, as they may be less likely to use such language in their pitches.

Moreover, research by Babson College's Center for Women's Entrepreneurial Leadership found that women entrepreneurs face challenges in accessing informal networks and resources such as mentorship and guidance, which can be crucial to business success.

This is due to factors such as lack of female role models, male-dominated industries, and a lack of awareness of available resources.

Overall, these studies suggest that gender bias and discrimination in the financial industry can contribute to challenges in access to funding and resources for women business owners.

Limited Representation: Women may be underrepresented in certain industries or fields, making it harder for them to find mentors, role models, and support networks.

The report by Catalyst titled "Women CEOs of the S&P 500" highlights the progress of women in attaining top leadership positions in the largest companies in the United States. As of 2018, women held 5.2% of CEO positions in the S&P 500, up from 4.8% in 2017. However, this still represents a significant gender gap in top leadership positions. The report also notes that women of color face even greater challenges in reaching leadership positions, with only one woman of color holding a CEO position in the S&P 500 at the time of the report.

Gender bias is a big issue that affects women both at work and in the marketplace, but we can make progress by learning more about its different forms and impacts. Despite these challenges, many successful women have found ways to overcome gender bias and achieve great things. For example, Oprah Winfrey faced discrimination and harassment as a young TV reporter, but she didn't let that stop her. Sara Blakely, the founder of Spanx, had to deal with negative feedback from male investors, but she stuck to her vision and built a successful business anyway.

These women's stories are a powerful reminder that with hard work and determination, we can overcome the obstacles in our way. By supporting each other and fighting against gender bias, we can create a more inclusive and equitable world for all.

Ruth Bader Ginsburg: Ginsburg was one of the first women to attend Harvard Law School and later went on to become the second female justice on the U.S. Supreme Court. Throughout her career, she faced numerous instances of gender bias, including being denied a clerkship because of her gender and being paid less than her male colleagues as a law professor. Despite these challenges, Ginsburg continued to fight for gender equality and became a powerful advocate for women's rights.

Oprah Winfrey: Winfrey is a media mogul and philanthropist who has faced gender and racial bias throughout her career. She was told that she was "unfit for TV" and was repeatedly passed over for jobs because of her race and gender. Despite these obstacles, she persevered and went on to become one of the most successful women in media.

Mary Barra: Barra is the CEO of General Motors and one of the few women to lead a major automaker. She has faced gender bias throughout her career, including being told that she would never be able to become a plant manager because she was a woman. Despite these challenges, Barra worked her way up through the ranks and became the first woman to lead a major global automaker.

Sara Blakely: Blakely is the founder of Spanx, a successful women's shapewear company. She faced gender bias early on in her career, with investors telling her that her idea was "silly" and that women would never buy her product. Despite these setbacks, Blakely persevered and went on to build a successful company that has revolutionized the shapewear industry.

Gender bias is an issue that affects individuals, organizations, and society as a whole. The workplace and marketplace are not exempt from these biases, and women continue to face significant challenges in accessing equal opportunities, resources, and fair compensation. It is important for organizations and individuals to recognize and address these biases to promote diversity, equity, and inclusion. By creating more inclusive and supportive environments, we can help ensure that everyone has an equal opportunity to succeed, regardless of their gender or any other personal characteristic. Together, we can work towards a more equitable future, where everyone has a fair chance to achieve their full potential.

As a woman in business potentially facing gender bias, you have access to awesome mindsets and tools to help you thrive. One key mindset is having a growth mindset and believing in yourself, which involves embracing challenges, seeking feedback, and persisting through obstacles. Building a supportive network of other women in business is also crucial, as they can provide encouragement, advice, and a sense of community.

In addition to mindset, knowledge is power when it comes to overcoming gender bias. Understanding how it manifests in the workplace and marketplace can help you develop effective strategies. Check out resources like books, podcasts, and workshops on topics such as unconscious bias, negotiation skills, and assertiveness. And don't forget the power of technology and social media to network, promote your business, and reach new markets.

With these tools, you can stand up for yourself and thrive as a woman in business, despite the challenges of gender bias. Don't let it hold you back – you've got this!

Mentorship programs: connecting with other successful women in your industry who have faced and overcome similar obstacles can be incredibly valuable in building your confidence and skillset.

Networking events: attending events and conferences that bring together like-minded women in business can help you build your network, find new opportunities, and learn from others.

Professional development courses: investing in courses or workshops to develop new skills or deepen your expertise in your field can help you build your confidence and feel more prepared to take on new challenges.

Support groups: joining a support group or community of women in business can provide a safe space to discuss challenges, share experiences, and receive support and encouragement.

Resources for understanding gender bias: educating yourself on the ways that gender bias can manifest in the workplace and in the marketplace can help you identify and address instances of bias when they occur.

Advocacy organizations: joining or supporting advocacy organizations that work to promote gender equity and diversity in the workplace can be a powerful way to make a difference and support the larger movement for change.

Building A Diverse and Inclusive Team and Workplace Culture

Creating a diverse and inclusive workplace is essential for the success of any business. A diverse and inclusive team brings a variety of perspectives, experiences, and ideas that can lead to innovative solutions and better decision-making. However, building a diverse and inclusive team requires intentional effort and a commitment to change.

According to a report by McKinsey & Company, "companies in the top quartile for gender or racial and ethnic diversity are more likely to have financial returns above their national industry medians." This demonstrates the importance of creating a diverse and inclusive workplace not only for social justice but also for the success of the business.

One way to build a diverse and inclusive team is to prioritize diversity in recruitment and hiring practices. This means actively seeking out candidates from different backgrounds and creating a hiring process that is inclusive and free from bias. There are various resources available to help companies implement these practices, such as unconscious bias training, diverse recruitment networks, and inclusive job descriptions.

Another crucial step is to create a workplace culture that is welcoming and inclusive for all employees. This involves creating policies and practices that prioritize equity, such as flexible work arrangements, fair pay, and opportunities for professional development.

One example of a company that prioritizes diversity and inclusion in the workplace is Salesforce.

They have created a Chief Equality Officer position and established a number of initiatives to promote diversity and inclusion, such as employee resource groups and programs to address pay equity.

"We believe that our workforce should reflect the diversity of our customers and the communities we serve," says Cindy Robbins, former Chief People Officer at Salesforce. "It's not just the right thing to do, but it's also good for business."

Creating a diverse and inclusive workplace also involves addressing and dismantling systemic barriers and biases that can prevent marginalized groups from achieving success. This means taking a critical look at existing policies and practices and actively working to create a more equitable and just workplace.

One way to address these systemic barriers is to implement diversity, equity, and inclusion training for all employees. This training can help create a shared understanding of the importance of diversity and inclusion and provide strategies for creating a more equitable workplace.

Another essential aspect of building a diverse and inclusive workplace is creating opportunities for marginalized groups to take on leadership roles and have their voices heard. This means actively seeking out and supporting the advancement of underrepresented groups within the company.

"Leadership should reflect the diversity of the workforce and the customer base," says Maria Colacurcio, CEO of Syndio. "That's the only way you can get the unique perspectives and ideas needed to succeed in today's diverse and dynamic business environment."

Finally, creating a diverse and inclusive workplace requires ongoing commitment and effort. It's not enough to make a few changes and then declare the work done. Creating a truly inclusive workplace involves ongoing education, training, and reflection.

"We believe that diversity and inclusion are not just nice-to-haves, but they are essential for the success of our company and for the well-being of our employees," says Beth Galetti, Senior Vice President of People at Amazon. "We are committed to ongoing learning and improvement in this area."

"Diversity is not about how we differ. Diversity is about embracing one another's uniqueness." - Ola Joseph

Imposter Syndrome and Self-Doubt

Have you ever experienced that nagging feeling that you don't deserve to be where you are in your career, that you're not good enough, or that you don't belong? This feeling is commonly referred to as imposter syndrome, and it's a challenge that many successful women have faced. Even some of the most accomplished CEOs have experienced this self-doubt.

I have personally dealt with imposter syndrome and self-doubt many times over in my life and career. At times, I found myself questioning my abilities and second-guessing my decisions, despite my achievements and expertise. It wasn't until I learned to recognize these feelings as imposter syndrome and understand that it's a common experience, especially for women in male-dominated fields, that I was able to overcome them.

Through my own journey, I've developed strategies and insights that I hope will help other women who may be struggling with imposter syndrome and self-doubt. I believe that by sharing our experiences and supporting one another, we can build a community of confident and empowered women who are capable of achieving their goals and making a positive impact in their industries.

I'm passionate about helping women overcome these barriers and unlocking their full potential, and I hope that my personal experience can inspire and encourage others to do the same.

According to Reshma Saujani in her article "I Have Imposter Syndrome. Here's How I Deal with It" published in Harvard Business Review, acknowledging your imposter feelings and realizing that everyone experiences them is the first step towards overcoming them.

Saujani recommends finding a support system, practicing self-compassion, and reframing negative thoughts as strategies to tackle imposter syndrome.

In another article published in Fast Company, Elizabeth Segran highlights the importance of recognizing imposter feelings as a common experience, rather than a personal failure. She suggests seeking out mentors, role models, and communities of peers who can provide encouragement and support. Segran also emphasizes the need to celebrate achievements and focus on progress, rather than perfection.

Self-doubt is another common challenge that can hold women back in business. Katty Kay and Claire Shipman discuss the impact of women's self-doubt in their article "The Confidence Gap" published in The Atlantic. Women often hold themselves back from pursuing opportunities and taking risks because of their lack of confidence, even when they are highly competent. Sheryl Sandberg, in her book "Lean In: Women, Work, and the Will to Lead," encourages women to believe in their abilities and push past their fears and insecurities.

Remember that every successful businesswoman has her own unique journey and strengths. Comparing yourself to others and feeling like you're not measuring up will only hold you back. Don't let imposter syndrome and self-doubt prevent you from reaching your full potential. Acknowledge your feelings, seek support and encouragement, and focus on celebrating your achievements and progress.

Boosting your confidence and overcoming imposter syndrome and self-doubt takes effort, but it's worth it.

Here are some strategies to help you:

First, take a moment to acknowledge your accomplishments. Make a list of your achievements, skills, and experiences. It's easy to focus on your weaknesses, but remember to also recognize your strengths and the hard work that went into achieving your goals.

Next, challenge negative self-talk. Pay attention to the negative thoughts that pop up in your head and question their validity. Instead of dwelling on your weaknesses, focus on solutions and ways to improve.

It's also important to seek support. Surround yourself with people who believe in you and your abilities. Find a mentor, join a networking group, or seek out a business coach to help you stay motivated and confident.

Don't forget to practice self-care. Taking care of your physical and mental health is crucial to boosting your confidence. Try to exercise regularly, get enough sleep, and practice relaxation techniques such as meditation or yoga.

Finally, take action. Don't let self-doubt hold you back from taking risks and pursuing your goals. Take small steps towards your goals every day and celebrate each achievement along the way. With practice and perseverance, you can overcome self-doubt and achieve success in business.

It's important to recognize that imposter syndrome and self-doubt are not uncommon among highly successful women in business. Despite external achievements, many women struggle with feelings of inadequacy or fear of being exposed as a fraud. But it's important to remember that these feelings are not a reflection of one's abilities or accomplishments.

To overcome imposter syndrome and self-doubt, it's helpful to reframe negative thoughts and beliefs. Acknowledge and celebrate your successes and remind yourself of the hard work and dedication that brought you to where you are today. Additionally, seeking out support from trusted friends, colleagues, or mentors can provide valuable perspective and encouragement.

It's also important to recognize that setbacks and failures are a natural part of the journey towards success. Embrace these challenges as opportunities for growth and learning, rather than evidence of your inadequacy.

Ultimately, the key to overcoming imposter syndrome and self-doubt is to practice self-compassion and remind yourself that you are deserving of success and respect. With time and perseverance, these negative feelings can be replaced with confidence and a strong sense of self-worth, paving the way for continued success in business and beyond.

"I have written eleven books, but each time I think, 'uh oh, they're going to find out now. I've run a game on everybody, and they're going to find me out.'" - Maya Angelou

Advocating for Oneself & Negotiating Effectively

Advocating for oneself and negotiating effectively are crucial skills for any leader, especially for women in business who may face additional challenges due to gender bias. One example of a successful woman who has advocated for herself and negotiated effectively is Mellody Hobson, Co-CEO of Ariel Investments. Hobson has spoken publicly about her experiences negotiating for her salary and benefits, as well as for better representation of women and people of color on company boards.

To become a more effective advocate and negotiator, it's important to understand the process and prepare in advance. This can include doing research on industry standards for salaries and benefits, anticipating objections or counterarguments, and practicing effective communication skills.

Resources for improving advocacy and negotiation skills include books such as "Getting to Yes: Negotiating Agreement Without Giving In" by Roger Fisher and William Ury, and "Ask for More: 10 Questions to Negotiate Anything" by Alexandra Carter. Online courses and webinars on negotiation skills are also available through platforms like LinkedIn Learning and Coursera.

It's important to note that advocating for oneself and negotiating effectively can be challenging, especially in male-dominated industries. However, these skills are essential for career advancement and can lead to positive changes not just for oneself, but for other women and underrepresented groups in the workplace.

Balancing Work & Family Responsibilities

As a working mother and entrepreneur, I know firsthand the challenges of balancing work and family responsibilities. I raised two children while holding down a full-time job and working on my business in my free time, often in the evenings and weekends when my musician husband was away. I understand the constant juggling act of managing schedules, priorities, and unexpected demands. But through this experience, I also learned the importance of setting boundaries, delegating tasks, and prioritizing self-care. I hope to share some of the strategies and lessons I have learned with other women who are navigating the complexities of work and family life.

Balancing work and family responsibilities can be a significant challenge for women in business, particularly for women who hold top leadership positions such as CEOs. Many women feel the pressure to excel in both their professional and personal lives, often leading to feelings of burnout and stress. Women often have additional responsibilities at home, including caring for children, elderly parents, or other family members. This can create a difficult balancing act between work and home life. Additionally, traditional gender roles and societal expectations can create barriers for women seeking to balance their work and family responsibilities. Women may face stigma or discrimination in the workplace if they prioritize their family obligations over work, while also feeling guilt or judgment from family members if they prioritize their career.

Ultimately, finding a balance between work and family responsibilities is crucial for women's success and well-being in business.

Finding the balance between work and family responsibilities can be a significant challenge for She CEOs.

However, there are strategies that can help them navigate this delicate balance successfully. According to Tory Burch, founder and CEO of her fashion brand, having a supportive team and a flexible schedule are essential components. In her interview with Shana Lebowitz for Business Insider, Burch stresses the importance of being present for both her children and her business. She also emphasizes the need for self-care and taking breaks to prevent burnout.

Additionally, in Jacqueline Whitmore's Entrepreneur article "CEO Moms Share Their Secrets to Work-Life Balance," Karen Clark Cole, co-founder and CEO of Blink UX, emphasizes the importance of being present in the moment and finding a support system that allows for flexibility. Meanwhile, Ashley Tyrner, founder and CEO of Farmbox Direct, prioritizes and organizes her day, writing everything down and ensuring that her kids come first, with work as a close second. Overall, balancing work and family responsibilities requires a combination of prioritization, organization, flexibility, and self-care.

Juggling work and family responsibilities can be a daunting task, especially for female CEOs who are leading their companies and managing households at the same time. With a multitude of tasks to handle and limited time to get everything done, it's easy to feel overwhelmed and stressed. However, with the right strategies and mindset, it is possible to achieve a healthy work-life balance. In this section, we will explore some tips and insights from successful female CEOs on how they manage to balance their personal and professional lives. These tips range from prioritizing self-care to building a strong support system and being present in the moment. By implementing these tips, female CEOs can take charge of their lives and achieve both personal and professional success.

Set priorities: It's important to establish your priorities and determine what's most important to you. This can help you make decisions about how to allocate your time and energy.

Delegate: As a CEO, it's crucial to delegate tasks to capable team members, especially those that are not within your core competencies. Doing so can help lighten your load and free up time for other responsibilities, such as spending quality time with your family. By delegating, you also empower your team to take on more responsibility and grow in their roles.

Create boundaries: Setting boundaries between work and home life is essential to avoid burnout and ensure that you're giving enough attention to both aspects of your life. You can create boundaries by having designated times when you're not available for work calls or emails or carving out specific family time each week. It's important to communicate these boundaries clearly with your team and family so that everyone is aware of your availability.

Use technology to your advantage: Technology can be an ally in helping you balance work and family responsibilities. Video conferencing can help you stay connected with your team even when you're not in the office, while project management software can help you keep track of tasks and deadlines. Scheduling apps can help you manage your time more efficiently and ensure that you don't overbook yourself. However, it's also important to be mindful of the amount of time you spend on technology and make sure that it doesn't interfere with your personal life.

Practice self-care: Taking care of yourself physically and mentally is essential to avoid burnout and maintain a healthy work-life balance. This can include exercise, meditation, therapy, or simply taking time to relax and recharge. Make sure to prioritize self-care activities in your schedule and don't neglect your physical and mental health in favor of work responsibilities. Remember that taking care of yourself is not only essential for your well-being but also for your ability to perform at your best as a CEO.

Seek support: Build a support network of family, friends, and colleagues who can help you manage both work and family responsibilities.

It's important to remember that achieving work-life balance is a continual process and may require adjustments over time. By being intentional and proactive about balancing work and family responsibilities, female CEOs can successfully manage both aspects of their lives.

"Work-life balance is not a women's issue, it's a societal issue. And, it will take all of us, men and women, working together to make change." - Arianna Huffington.

Managing Difficult Conversations & Conflicts in The Workplace

Effective communication is key to success in any business, but sometimes, conversations can be difficult or uncomfortable. As a She CEO, it's important to know how to navigate these situations and handle conflicts with grace and professionalism.

One example of a difficult conversation is giving negative feedback to an employee. It's important to approach this type of conversation with empathy and a focus on solutions. As author and leadership expert Simon Sinek says, "Leadership is not about being in charge. It's about taking care of those in your charge." This means that as a leader, it's your responsibility to provide constructive feedback that helps your employee improve.

Another example of a difficult conversation is addressing conflicts between team members. This can be especially challenging if the conflict is due to personal differences or misunderstandings. In these situations, it's important to remain neutral and focus on finding a solution that benefits everyone involved. As conflict resolution expert Dana Caspersen notes, "Conflict is a natural part of life. It can be an opportunity for growth and learning, or it can be destructive. The difference lies in how we handle it."

To effectively manage difficult conversations and conflicts, it's important to have strong communication and conflict resolution skills. Here are some resources and tips to help:

Practice active listening: This means fully focusing on the person speaking and seeking to understand their perspective. Author Stephen Covey notes, "Most people do not listen with the intent to understand; they listen with the intent to reply." By actively listening, you can better understand the other person's point of view and find common ground.

Use "I" statements: When addressing conflicts or giving feedback, it's important to use "I" statements to express your own thoughts and feelings. For example, instead of saying "You're not meeting expectations," say "I'm concerned about the progress on this project and how we can improve it."

Focus on solutions: Instead of dwelling on the problem, focus on finding a solution that benefits everyone involved. As management expert Ken Blanchard notes, "There's a difference between interest and commitment. When you're interested in doing something, you do it only when it's convenient. When you're committed to something, you accept no excuses, only results." By committing to finding a solution, you can help your team move forward and grow.

Seek outside help if needed: Sometimes, conflicts or difficult conversations require the help of a third party, such as a mediator or HR representative. Don't hesitate to seek outside help if needed to ensure that conflicts are resolved in a fair and professional manner.

By developing strong communication and conflict resolution skills, you can effectively manage difficult conversations and conflicts in the workplace, ultimately creating a more positive and productive work environment for everyone involved.

> *"The difference between successful people and others is how long they spend time feeling sorry for themselves."* - Barbara Corcoran

Developing A Strong Personal Brand & Online Presence

In today's digital age, having a strong personal brand and online presence is essential for success as a She CEO. Your personal brand is how you represent yourself to the world and how you differentiate yourself from others in your industry. Building a strong personal brand can help you establish credibility, gain recognition, and attract new opportunities.

One key aspect of building a strong personal brand is developing a clear and consistent message that communicates who you are, what you do, and what sets you apart. This message should be reflected in your online presence, including your website, social media profiles, and other online platforms.

Creating and maintaining a strong online presence can also help you expand your network and build relationships with potential clients, investors, and collaborators. By sharing your expertise and insights on social media and other platforms, you can establish yourself as a thought leader in your industry and attract new opportunities.

There are many resources available to help you build a strong personal brand and online presence. Here are a few tips and resources to get you started:

Define your personal brand message: What do you want to be known for? What are your values and mission as a She CEO? Develop a clear and concise message that communicates your unique value proposition.

Create a professional website: Your website is your digital storefront and should reflect your personal brand message. Use a clean and modern design that is easy to navigate, and make sure your contact information is easy to find.

Develop a content strategy: Identify the topics and themes that are relevant to your personal brand message and develop a content strategy that includes blog posts, social media posts, and other types of content.

Use social media strategically: Choose the social media platforms that are most relevant to your audience and industry, and use them to share your content and engage with others in your network. Use hashtags and other tools to expand your reach and connect with new people.

Monitor and manage your online reputation: Regularly monitor your online presence to ensure that your personal brand message is consistent and accurate. Use tools like Google Alerts to monitor mentions of your name or brand online, and respond promptly to any negative feedback or criticism.

Here are a few additional resources that can help you build a strong personal brand and online presence:

- "The Brand Called You" by Tom Peters (Fast Company)
- "Personal Branding for Entrepreneurs" by Neil Patel
- "Building a Personal Brand: A Primer for Emerging Leaders" (Harvard Business Review)

By developing a strong personal brand and online presence, you can establish yourself as a leader in your industry and attract new opportunities for growth and success.

Overcoming Funding Challenges: Strategies for She CEOs

As a She CEO, one of the biggest challenges you may face is getting access to funding and capital. It's a tough challenge to overcome in the business world, especially for women entrepreneurs. I completely understand the struggle of finding funding and accessing capital to grow your business, as I faced similar obstacles when I started my own business. Despite the odds stacked against me, I was determined to make my dream a reality. However, looking back, I realize that I made mistakes in my approach to funding and capital.

That's why I'm passionate about helping other She CEOs find funding and access capital in the right way. By seeking out the right resources, building strong relationships with investors and lenders, and having a solid business plan in place, we can secure the funding needed to achieve our goals and grow our businesses in a sustainable way. As **Roberta** Matuson, a leadership coach and consultant, advises, women entrepreneurs should seek out investors and lenders who specifically support women-led businesses and prepare an effective pitch to win them over.

A report by the National Women's Business Council revealed that women entrepreneurs face persistent disparities when it comes to accessing capital and funding, as compared to their male counterparts. However, there are various options available, including traditional funding sources, alternative financing strategies, and organizations dedicated to supporting women-led businesses.

Women entrepreneurs can consider exploring a range of funding and capital options, including venture capital, angel investors, crowdfunding, and small business loans.

Apart from these, they can also look into alternative financing strategies like microloans, grants, and partnerships. For instance, the Tory Burch Foundation provides loans, education, and mentorship to women entrepreneurs, and the Women's Business Center offers training, counseling, and funding opportunities for women entrepreneurs.

Despite these options, the biggest challenge for women entrepreneurs is to access venture capital, which is the primary source of funding for many startups. According to PitchBook, in 2019, women-led startups received only 2.8% of venture capital funding. This number highlights the significant gender gap in funding and capital access. However, organizations like the Women's Venture Capital Fund and All Raise are working to increase the number of women investors and venture capitalists, thus reducing the gender gap in funding and capital access.

Access to funding and capital is a crucial challenge for women entrepreneurs, but with the right resources, networking, and pitching skills, it's a challenge that can be overcome. Women entrepreneurs can explore various funding and capital options, including alternative financing strategies and organizations dedicated to supporting women-led businesses. Additionally, the increasing number of women investors and venture capitalists is a positive sign that the gender gap in funding and capital access may reduce over time.

Maintaining Work-Life Balance & Avoiding Burnout

Maintaining a healthy work-life balance is essential for success and overall well-being as a She CEO. Juggling multiple responsibilities and demands can quickly lead to burnout, which can negatively impact both personal and professional life. In this section, we'll explore strategies for maintaining work-life balance and avoiding burnout.

One key strategy is to set boundaries and prioritize self-care. This may include scheduling regular breaks throughout the day, taking time off for vacations or personal days, and engaging in activities that bring joy and relaxation outside of work. As She CEO Dr. Amina AlTai advises, "Self-care is not a luxury. It's a non-negotiable."

Another important aspect is to manage time effectively and delegate tasks when necessary. This can involve assessing which tasks require your personal attention and which can be handled by others on your team. As She CEO of The Riveter Amy Nelson notes, "It's not about doing everything yourself. It's about building a great team that you trust and delegating effectively so that everyone can thrive."

In addition, it's important to cultivate a supportive work environment that values work-life balance. This may involve offering flexible schedules or remote work options, promoting mental health resources, and encouraging employees to prioritize their well-being. As She CEO of TELUS International, Marilyn Tyfting emphasizes, "It's about creating a culture where employees feel valued and supported."

Finally, staying connected with friends, family, and a wider community can also help maintain work-life balance and prevent burnout. This can include participating in social events and hobbies, volunteering, and engaging in mentorship or networking opportunities.

Overall, maintaining work-life balance and avoiding burnout is essential for personal and professional success. By prioritizing self-care, managing time effectively, cultivating a supportive work environment, and staying connected with community, She CEOs can achieve a fulfilling and sustainable balance in their lives.

"Almost everything will work again if you unplug it for a few minutes, including you." - Anne Lamott.

Staying Up to Date with Industry Trends and Innovations

As a She CEO, it's important to stay informed about the latest trends and innovations in your industry. This allows you to make informed decisions, adapt to changes, and stay ahead of the competition. Here are some tips to help you stay up to date:

Attend industry events and conferences: Attending events and conferences relevant to your industry is a great way to stay informed about the latest trends, innovations, and best practices. You can also network with other professionals and learn from their experiences.

Follow thought leaders and influencers: Following thought leaders and influencers in your industry on social media and other platforms can provide valuable insights and ideas. They often share their thoughts on the latest trends and offer advice on how to stay ahead of the curve.

Join industry associations and organizations: Joining industry associations and organizations can help you stay connected with other professionals and stay up to date on industry news and trends. Many organizations also offer training and development opportunities that can help you grow as a leader.

Read industry publications and blogs: Industry publications and blogs are great resources for staying up to date on the latest trends and innovations. They often feature articles written by experts in the field and offer insights and analysis on the latest developments.

Collaborate with other businesses: Collaborating with other businesses in your industry can be a great way to stay up to date on the latest trends and innovations. You can share ideas, knowledge, and experiences to help each other grow and succeed.

One great example of staying up to date with industry trends is the company Amazon. Amazon has been able to maintain its status as a dominant player in the retail industry by constantly adapting to new trends and innovations. For example, when e-commerce began to gain popularity, Amazon quickly embraced it and became one of the largest online retailers in the world. More recently, Amazon has been investing heavily in artificial intelligence and machine learning to improve its operations and customer experience.

Another example is the fashion industry, which is constantly evolving with new trends and styles. Fashion designers and brands must stay up to date with the latest trends in order to remain relevant and successful. One example of a designer who has successfully adapted to changing trends is Diane von Furstenberg. She is known for her iconic wrap dress, but has also expanded her brand to include other styles and products to stay current with evolving fashion trends.

Building Resilience and Coping with Failure

As a She CEO, building resilience and learning to cope with failure are essential to success. Failure is inevitable, and setbacks are a part of the journey. However, it's how you respond to these challenges that will set you apart as a leader.

Resilience is the ability to bounce back from adversity and maintain a positive outlook in the face of challenges. It's about staying focused on your goals and persevering through difficult times. According to Resilience.org, "Resilience is not just the ability to bounce back from adversity; it is the ability to grow and learn from it."

One way to build resilience is to reframe your mindset around failure. Instead of seeing failure as a negative experience, view it as an opportunity for growth and learning.

As Oprah Winfrey once said, *"Think like a queen. A queen is not afraid to fail. Failure is another stepping stone to greatness."*

Another way to build resilience is to cultivate a strong support system. This includes not only your personal relationships but also your professional network. Surround yourself with people who will support and encourage you during tough times.

Coping with failure also requires self-care practices to avoid burnout. Burnout can happen when you're constantly pushing yourself to the limit without taking breaks or engaging in self-care. According to the World Health Organization, "Burn-out is a syndrome conceptualized as resulting from chronic workplace stress that has not been successfully managed."

To avoid burnout, it's important to prioritize self-care. This can include things like exercise, meditation, and spending time with loved ones. Taking breaks and vacations are also important for maintaining a healthy work-life balance.

Let's look at how some successful women in business have built resilience and coped with failure. For instance, take Sara Blakely, the founder of Spanx. Despite failing the LSAT twice and working multiple jobs, Blakely didn't give up. Instead, she took the leap to start her own business at the age of 29. Blakely attributes her success to her willingness to take risks and not let the fear of failure hold her back. Her story serves as a reminder that setbacks and failures are a natural part of any journey, and that it's how we respond to those challenges that truly defines us.

Another example is Mary Barra, CEO of General Motors. Barra faced criticism for her handling of the company's 2014 recall crisis, but she refused to let it defeat her. Instead, she focused on addressing the issues and moving forward.

There are plenty of resources available to help you build resilience and learn how to cope with failure. Two great books to check out are "Option B" by Sheryl Sandberg and Adam Grant and "The Resilience Factor" by Karen Reivich and Andrew Shatte. The American Psychological Association also has a helpful webpage called "Building Your Resilience" that provides tips and strategies for developing resilience. Additionally, the Resilience.org website offers a wealth of information and resources on building resilience and overcoming challenges. These are just a few examples of the many resources available to help you develop your resilience and cope with failure.

Building resilience and learning to cope with failure are essential for success as a She CEO. Reframe your mindset around failure, cultivate a strong support system, prioritize self-care, and learn from real-life examples of successful women in business. Remember, failure is not the opposite of success, but rather a part of the journey to achieving it.

From Challenge to Opportunity: Embracing the SHE CEO Mindset

While the challenges women face in business can be daunting, there are many strategies and resources available to help women overcome these obstacles and thrive as She CEOs. By developing leadership skills, cultivating resilience, building a strong network, advocating for oneself, and staying up-to-date with industry trends, women can successfully navigate the unique challenges they face and achieve their goals.

It is important to remember that building a successful career as a She CEO is a journey, and there will inevitably be setbacks and challenges along the way. But by maintaining a growth mindset and a willingness to learn and adapt, women can turn these challenges into opportunities for growth and success.

As a She CEO, it is also important to prioritize self-care and work-life balance in order to avoid burnout and maintain overall well-being. By cultivating a culture of respect and inclusivity in the workplace and promoting diversity and equity, women can create an environment that supports the success and well-being of all team members.

The challenges women face in business are real, but with the right strategies, resources, and mindset, women can overcome these obstacles and thrive as She CEOs. By continuing to develop skills and knowledge, building strong networks, and advocating for oneself, women can achieve success and inspire others to do the same.

As we conclude Chapter 2 on " The Challenges Women Face in Business," it's important to reflect on the challenges and biases that women face in the workplace.

We've explored strategies for overcoming these obstacles and achieving success, but it's also important to continue the conversation and push for progress. To further stimulate your thinking and encourage self-reflection, we've provided some thought-provoking questions for you to consider.

❖ Have you ever faced imposter syndrome or self-doubt in your professional life? How did you overcome it?

❖ What are some ways in which you can develop a growth mindset and continue to learn and grow in your career?

❖ How do you currently prioritize and balance your personal and professional responsibilities? Is there room for improvement?

❖ What are some strategies you can use to overcome obstacles and challenges in your career, both internal and external?

❖ How can you cultivate a sense of purpose and mission in your work, and how might this inspire and motivate you?

CHAPTER 3

The Characteristics of Successful Women in Business

"Define success on your own terms, achieve it by your own rules, and build a life you're proud to live." - Anne Sweeney

As we embark on this journey of exploring the characteristics of successful women in business, I can't help but feel excited about the dynamic and inspiring women we'll encounter along the way. From fearless risk-takers to savvy strategists, these women have broken down barriers and shattered glass ceilings to make their mark in the business world. I hope that through their stories, we can all feel inspired, empowered, and energized to pursue our own success in business. So, let's dive in and learn what it takes to be a successful SHE CEO!

Women in business face a unique set of challenges and obstacles, but those who succeed often share certain characteristics that set them apart. One of the most critical traits is resilience. As Liz Elting, CEO of the Elizabeth Elting Foundation, notes, "Resilience is critical for anyone, but especially for women in business, who face unique challenges and often have to work harder than their male counterparts to get ahead."

Research supports this notion. A study by McKinsey & Company found that "women remain significantly underrepresented in the workforce and that gender inequality persists across all dimensions of diversity." The study also found that companies with diverse leadership teams, including women in executive positions, tend to perform better financially.

Another critical characteristic of successful women in business is a willingness to take risks. As Jody Miller, CEO of Business Talent Group, notes, "Women who succeed in business are willing to take risks, even when it's uncomfortable or scary. They recognize that failure is a natural part of the process and that taking calculated risks can lead to significant rewards."

Finally, successful women in business tend to be highly adaptable. As the business landscape changes rapidly, those who can adapt quickly are more likely to succeed.

As Annette King, CEO of Publicis Groupe UK, notes, "Adaptability is critical in today's fast-paced business world. Women who can adapt quickly to changing circumstances are more likely to succeed, as they can pivot quickly and take advantage of new opportunities."

Successful women in business often share certain characteristics, including resilience, a willingness to take risks, and adaptability. These traits help women navigate the unique challenges and obstacles they face in the business world and succeed despite the odds. By developing and cultivating these traits, women can increase their chances of success in business.

Leadership Skills and Management Styles

I understand firsthand the importance of strong leadership skills and effective management styles in building and growing a successful business. In the early days of my own business, I found myself wearing multiple hats and trying to juggle all aspects of the business on my own. It was a steep learning curve, and I soon realized that I needed to develop my leadership skills and delegate responsibilities to a capable team if I wanted to take my business to the next level.

Working with a business coach and assembling a strong team were game-changers for my business. It wasn't an overnight process, but with time and effort, we were able to build a cohesive team that shared my vision and was equipped to handle the day-to-day operations of the business. Today, I'm proud to say that my business is thriving and continuing to grow, thanks in no small part to the leadership skills and management styles we've developed as a team. Leadership skills and management styles are crucial for any business to thrive and succeed, and women entrepreneurs are no exception.

Effective leadership skills enable women to inspire, motivate, and guide their teams towards achieving the organization's goals. While management styles can vary, there are certain characteristics that are commonly associated with successful women leaders.

One critical aspect of effective leadership is emotional intelligence. Emotional intelligence refers to the ability to recognize, understand, and manage one's emotions and those of others. It enables leaders to empathize with their team members, communicate effectively, and build strong relationships. According to a study by the Harvard Business Review, "emotional intelligence accounts for nearly 90 percent of what moves people up the ladder when IQ and technical skills are roughly similar."

Another essential characteristic of successful women leaders is the ability to be adaptable and flexible. In today's rapidly changing business environment, adaptability is critical to staying ahead of the competition. As Kathryn Minshew, founder of The Muse, states, "you have to be able to pivot, change directions, and make tough decisions quickly."

Effective communication skills are also essential for successful women leaders. Communication skills enable leaders to clearly articulate their vision, goals, and expectations to their team members. It also enables them to listen actively and provide feedback, creating a culture of open communication within the organization.

In addition to these essential leadership skills, successful women entrepreneurs also have distinct management styles. Some women entrepreneurs may adopt a collaborative management style, which emphasizes teamwork and consensus-building.

This style is effective in promoting innovation, encouraging participation and feedback, and empowering team members. Other women entrepreneurs may adopt a directive management style, which is more authoritative and task-focused. This style is effective in situations where quick decisions and a clear direction are required.

One study conducted by the Peterson Institute for International Economics found that companies with a higher percentage of women in top management positions have a higher profitability margin compared to those with a lower percentage of women in top management.

The study also found that companies with diverse leadership teams had better employee engagement and retention rates.

Another study by the National Bureau of Economic Research found that women-led companies outperformed male-led companies, generating higher revenues and delivering stronger returns on investment. The study also found that women-led companies were more likely to adopt innovative practices and invest in research and development.

In summary, effective leadership skills and management styles are crucial for the success of women entrepreneurs. Emotional intelligence, adaptability, and effective communication skills are essential leadership skills that enable women entrepreneurs to inspire and motivate their teams. Additionally, collaborative and directive management styles can be effective in different situations. Research has shown that companies with diverse leadership teams and women-led companies tend to have higher profitability margins, better employee engagement and retention rates, and are more likely to adopt innovative practices.

Resilience And Determination

Resilience and determination are crucial traits for She CEOs to possess. In the face of adversity and setbacks, resilience and determination allow women entrepreneurs to persevere and succeed in their endeavors.

Research has shown that resilience is a key factor in entrepreneurial success. A study published in the International Journal of Entrepreneurial Behavior and Research found that resilience is positively associated with entrepreneurial success and that entrepreneurs with high levels of resilience are better able to cope with the challenges and uncertainties of starting and growing a business.

In addition to resilience, determination is also a critical trait for She CEOs. Determination is the ability to persist and pursue goals in the face of obstacles and challenges. It allows women entrepreneurs to stay focused on their vision and work towards achieving their goals, even when faced with setbacks and difficulties.

According to a study by the Centre for Entrepreneurs, determination is one of the most important traits for successful entrepreneurs. The study found that determination is essential for overcoming the challenges of starting and growing a business and that it is a key factor in achieving entrepreneurial success.

One example of a successful She CEO who embodies resilience and determination is Sara Blakely, the founder of Spanx. Blakely faced multiple rejections and setbacks when trying to launch her business, but she persisted and eventually created a multi-billion dollar brand.

In an interview with Forbes, Blakely credited her success to her ability to embrace failure and stay resilient in the face of challenges. "I failed my way to success," she said. "I learned to be comfortable with failure and to not take it personally. I realized that every 'no' was getting me closer to a 'yes'."

Another example is Jennifer Hyman, the co-founder and CEO of Rent the Runway. Hyman faced numerous challenges when launching her business, including skepticism from investors and technical difficulties with the company's website. However, she remained determined and persistent in pursuing her vision for the company.

In an interview with Entrepreneur, Hyman emphasized the importance of resilience and determination in entrepreneurship. "The ability to keep pushing forward when the going gets tough is critical," she said. "You have to be able to weather the ups and downs and stay focused on your goals."

So, how can She CEOs develop and strengthen their resilience and determination? One approach is to practice mindfulness and self-care. Taking time for self-reflection and self-care can help women entrepreneurs stay focused and centered in the face of challenges and setbacks.

Another approach is to surround oneself with a supportive network of peers, mentors, and allies. Having a community of support can provide women entrepreneurs with the encouragement and motivation they need to stay resilient and determined in pursuing their goals.

Resilience and determination are critical traits for She CEOs to possess.

Research has shown that resilience is positively associated with entrepreneurial success, while determination is essential for overcoming the challenges of starting and growing a business. Successful She CEOs like Sara Blakely and Jennifer Hyman embody these traits and have achieved tremendous success as a result. Developing resilience and determination can be accomplished through mindfulness and self-care and by building a supportive network of peers, mentors, and allies.

Creativity And Innovation

As a She CEO, creativity and innovation are key to driving success in your business. By thinking outside the box and finding new solutions to old problems, you can stay ahead of the competition and build a thriving business.

One way to cultivate creativity and innovation is to encourage your team to embrace new ideas and take risks. As Diane von Furstenberg, founder of the fashion brand DVF, puts it, "Innovation is about taking risks and trying new things. You have to be comfortable with failure to innovate." By creating a culture where experimentation and failure are seen as learning opportunities, you can empower your team to take risks and come up with innovative solutions.

Another way to foster creativity and innovation is to stay on top of industry trends and emerging technologies. As Martha Stewart, founder of Martha Stewart Living Omnimedia, notes, "You have to stay on top of trends, understand what's going on in your industry, and be willing to innovate." By keeping an eye on what's happening in your industry and experimenting with new technologies and approaches, you can stay ahead of the curve and drive innovation in your business.

It's also important to take the time to explore new ideas and pursue creative endeavors outside of work. As Sophia Amoruso, founder of Nasty Gal, points out, "Creativity is like a muscle – you have to exercise it to keep it strong." By engaging in creative pursuits like art, music, or writing, you can keep your mind sharp and bring fresh ideas and perspectives to your business.

Of course, it's important to balance creativity and innovation with practical considerations like budget and timeline constraints.

As Tory Burch, founder of the fashion brand Tory Burch, notes, "You can't just be creative. You have to be practical and have a business sense." By finding ways to channel your creativity in a way that aligns with your business goals and limitations, you can harness the power of innovation to drive your business forward.

In summary, as a She CEO, creativity and innovation are key to driving success in your business. By creating a culture that encourages risk-taking and experimentation, staying on top of industry trends and emerging technologies, pursuing creative endeavors outside of work, and balancing creativity with practical considerations, you can foster a culture of innovation and drive your business to new heights.

Networking And Collaboration

Networking and collaboration are essential components for any successful business, but they are especially important for women entrepreneurs. The ability to connect with others and form partnerships can help women entrepreneurs to expand their businesses, access new opportunities, and gain valuable insights and knowledge. In this section, we will discuss the importance of networking and collaboration for women entrepreneurs and provide tips and strategies for building and maintaining effective business relationships.

Networking and collaboration are crucial for women entrepreneurs in several ways. First, they can help women entrepreneurs to access new resources, such as funding, expertise, and talent. By connecting with other entrepreneurs, investors, and industry leaders, women entrepreneurs can gain valuable insights into market trends and opportunities, and develop new business strategies and ideas. Additionally, networking and collaboration can help women entrepreneurs to build their brand, increase their visibility, and establish themselves as thought leaders in their industry.

Second, networking and collaboration can provide women entrepreneurs with emotional support and motivation. Running a business can be stressful and challenging, and having a network of supportive peers and mentors can help women entrepreneurs to stay motivated and resilient in the face of obstacles and setbacks.

Third, networking and collaboration can help women entrepreneurs to overcome some of the unique challenges they face in the business world.

For example, women entrepreneurs often face gender-based biases and discrimination, and networking and collaboration can help them to connect with others who have faced similar challenges and can offer guidance and support. *Here are a few additional tips:*

Attend Industry Events and Conferences: Attending industry events and conferences is an excellent way for women entrepreneurs to network and connect with others in their industry. These events provide opportunities to meet other entrepreneurs, investors, and industry leaders, and learn about new developments and trends in the field. Many conferences also offer workshops and seminars on business topics, providing valuable learning opportunities for women entrepreneurs.

Join Professional Organizations: Joining professional organizations can provide women entrepreneurs with access to a network of peers and mentors in their industry. Many professional organizations offer networking events, mentorship programs, and other resources to help women entrepreneurs grow and succeed in their businesses.

Connect with Influencers on Social Media: Social media platforms such as LinkedIn, Twitter, and Instagram can be powerful tools for networking and building relationships with influencers and industry leaders. By following and engaging with influential people in their industry, women entrepreneurs can gain valuable insights and information, and establish themselves as thought leaders in their field.

Collaborate with Other Entrepreneurs: Collaborating with other entrepreneurs on projects or initiatives can be a great way for women entrepreneurs to build relationships and expand their networks.

By working with others, women entrepreneurs can leverage their combined expertise and resources to achieve common goals and build their businesses.

Seek Out Mentors and Advisors: Having a mentor or advisor can be invaluable for women entrepreneurs, providing them with guidance, support, and valuable insights into the business world. Women entrepreneurs can seek out mentors through professional organizations, networking events, and other channels.

Networking and collaboration are essential components for success in the business world, and they are especially important for women entrepreneurs. By building and maintaining strong business relationships, women entrepreneurs can access new resources, gain valuable insights and knowledge, and establish themselves as thought leaders in their industry.

Passion And Purpose

Passion and purpose are two driving forces that can propel a woman entrepreneur to success. When a woman has a clear sense of her passion and purpose, she can align her business goals with her personal values, creating a sense of fulfillment that drives her to succeed.

Passion is the driving force behind any successful business, and it is what sets successful women entrepreneurs apart from the rest. As Christine Lagarde, Managing Director of the International Monetary Fund, said, "Passion is not just an emotion, it is a force that can drive individuals and organizations to achieve extraordinary things."

When a woman is passionate about her business, she is more likely to put in the time and effort needed to make it successful.

But passion alone is not enough. As Steve Jobs once said, "I'm convinced that about half of what separates successful entrepreneurs from the non-successful ones is pure perseverance." This is where purpose comes in. Purpose gives a woman entrepreneur a clear sense of direction and a reason to persevere when things get tough.

Purpose can also inspire employees and customers to get on board with a company's mission. As Richard Branson, founder of the Virgin Group, said, "A company is people... employees want to know... what's the point?" When a woman entrepreneur has a clear purpose for her business, she can communicate that purpose to her team and inspire them to work towards a common goal.

In addition to providing a sense of direction and motivation, passion and purpose can also help a woman entrepreneur make tough decisions.

When faced with a difficult choice, a woman can refer back to her passion and purpose to guide her decision-making process.

Passion and purpose can also help a woman entrepreneur overcome obstacles and persevere through tough times. As Arianna Huffington, founder of The Huffington Post, said, "We need to accept that we won't always make the right decisions, that we'll screw up royally sometimes - understanding that failure is not the opposite of success, it's part of success."

In order to find and pursue passion and purpose in business, women entrepreneurs can start by asking themselves some key questions.

- What do I care deeply about?
- What are my values and beliefs?
- What are their long-term goals for my business, and how do those goals align with my personal values?

By answering these questions, women entrepreneurs can begin to clarify their passion and purpose and align their business with those values.

It's important to note that passion and purpose do not guarantee success in business. Hard work, determination, and a willingness to take risks are also critical factors. However, when combined with these other qualities, passion and purpose can help a woman entrepreneur create a successful and fulfilling business.

Passion and purpose are key ingredients for success as a woman entrepreneur. By finding and pursuing their passions and aligning their businesses with their personal values, women entrepreneurs can create a sense of fulfillment and motivation that will help drive them to success. As Nelson Mandela once said, "There is no passion to be found playing small - in settling for a life that is less than the one you are capable of living." By pursuing their passions and purpose, women entrepreneurs can create the lives and businesses they are truly capable of living.

Emotional Intelligence

Emotional intelligence (EI) is a critical trait for successful leadership, particularly for She CEOs. EI involves the ability to recognize, understand, and manage one's own emotions while also being aware of and sensitive to the emotions of others. A high level of EI can help She CEOs create a positive and productive workplace culture, build strong relationships with employees and stakeholders, and navigate challenging situations with grace and effectiveness.

One real-life example of a She CEO with strong emotional intelligence is Mary Barra, the CEO of General Motors. Barra's leadership style emphasizes collaboration, transparency, and empathy, and she has made significant efforts to improve GM's workplace culture, including implementing a program to address sexual harassment and discrimination.

To develop emotional intelligence, She CEOs can work on several key skills, including:

Self-awareness: This involves recognizing and understanding one's own emotions, strengths, and weaknesses. She CEOs can improve self-awareness by practicing mindfulness, journaling, or seeking feedback from others.

Self-regulation: This involves managing one's own emotions, particularly in challenging or high-pressure situations. She CEOs can improve self-regulation by practicing relaxation techniques, such as deep breathing or meditation, and developing a strong support network of friends, family, and mentors.

Empathy: This involves understanding and being sensitive to the emotions and needs of others.

She CEOs can improve empathy by actively listening to others, considering different perspectives, and seeking to understand the experiences of people from diverse backgrounds.

Social skills: This involves building strong relationships and effective communication with others. She CEOs can improve social skills by practicing active listening, giving and receiving feedback, and seeking opportunities for collaboration and teamwork.

There are many resources available to help She CEOs develop emotional intelligence, including books such as "Emotional Intelligence 2.0" by Travis Bradberry and Jean Greaves and "Primal Leadership: Realizing the Power of Emotional Intelligence" by Daniel Goleman, Richard Boyatzis, and Annie McKee. She CEOs can also attend workshops or seminars on emotional intelligence, such as those offered by the Emotional Intelligence Academy or the Institute for Social + Emotional Intelligence.

Emotional intelligence is a crucial trait for She CEOs, and developing this skill can help improve workplace culture, build strong relationships, and navigate difficult situations with effectiveness and empathy. By practicing self-awareness, self-regulation, empathy, and social skills, She CEOs can become more emotionally intelligent leaders and drive success in their businesses.

Flexibility and Adaptability

As a She CEO, you will undoubtedly face unexpected challenges and changes in your business. To succeed, it is essential to remain flexible and adaptable. Being open to change can help you to stay ahead of the curve and remain competitive in your industry.

One example of a She CEO who exemplifies flexibility and adaptability is Ginni Rometty, the former CEO of IBM. During her tenure, Rometty transformed the company's focus from hardware to cloud computing, data analytics, and AI. She emphasized the importance of adapting to the rapidly changing technology landscape, stating, "Never love something so much that you can't let go of it."

Another example is Rosalind Brewer, the CEO of Walgreens Boots Alliance. In 2020, when the COVID-19 pandemic hit, Brewer quickly adapted her business strategy, increasing delivery options and expanding partnerships to offer more testing and vaccinations. She emphasized the importance of agility, stating, "We need to be agile, we need to be fast, and we need to have the ability to pivot."

Consider these for cultivating flexibility and adaptability:

- Stay informed about industry trends and changes.
- Encourage a culture of innovation and experimentation in your business.
- Foster a growth mindset in yourself and your team.
- Learn from failures and use them as opportunities for growth and improvement.
- Build a diverse and inclusive team to bring new perspectives and ideas.

"The only constant in business is change. The companies that can adapt are the ones that will thrive."- Mark Cuban

Financial Acumen

As a She CEO, it is crucial to have a strong understanding of financial management and business operations. While this may not be a skillset that comes naturally to everyone, it is essential to develop financial acumen to ensure the success and longevity of your business.

Financial acumen refers to the ability to understand and interpret financial statements, budgets, and other financial data. It also involves the ability to make informed decisions based on this information to optimize financial performance and achieve business goals.

One of the primary reasons why financial acumen is essential for She CEOs is that it helps to inform critical business decisions. Having a strong understanding of your company's financials can help you make informed decisions on issues such as pricing, budget allocation, and investments.

Another benefit of having financial acumen is that it can help you identify potential areas of financial risk and make proactive changes to mitigate them. This can help you avoid financial pitfalls and ensure the long-term success of your business.

Many successful women in business have demonstrated exceptional financial acumen, and their stories can be inspiring and instructive. One such example is Sara Blakely, founder of Spanx.

Blakely started her company with just $5,000 and a lot of determination. She was determined to keep control of the company and avoided taking on investors for many years.

She also made strategic decisions about where to invest her resources, such as focusing on product development rather than expensive advertising campaigns. Today, Spanx is a household name and a multi-million-dollar company.

Another example is Indra Nooyi, former CEO of PepsiCo. Nooyi was instrumental in transforming PepsiCo's product lineup to include healthier options, which ultimately led to increased profitability. She also prioritized corporate social responsibility and made significant investments in sustainable business practices.

"Financial acumen is essential for any business leader. It enables you to make informed decisions, minimize financial risk, and maximize profitability." - Ursula Burns, former CEO of Xerox

If you want to improve your financial acumen as a She CEO, there are many resources available to you. Here are a few options to consider:

Financial management courses: Many universities and business schools offer courses in financial management that can help you develop a strong understanding of financial statements, budgeting, and other essential financial concepts.

Business books: There are many excellent books available on financial management and business operations, including "Financial Intelligence" by Karen Berman and Joe Knight, "The Lean CFO" by Nicholas Katko, and "Financial Statements" by Thomas Ittelson.

Industry associations: Joining industry associations can provide you with access to networking opportunities, industry-specific knowledge, and educational resources.

Financial acumen is a critical skillset for She CEOs. By developing a strong understanding of financial management and business operations, you can make informed decisions, minimize financial risk, and maximize profitability.

Look for opportunities to learn and grow your financial acumen, and don't be afraid to seek out the advice of financial experts when needed. With dedication and hard work, you can become a financially savvy She CEO and drive the success of your business.

"Financial acumen is not about being a math genius. It's about having a basic understanding of finance and being able to use that knowledge to make informed business decisions." - Beth Mooney, former CEO of KeyCorp

Entrepreneurial Spirit

Entrepreneurship is not just a career path, but a mindset and approach to life. Successful She CEOs possess an entrepreneurial spirit, which is characterized by innovation, risk-taking, and a willingness to learn and adapt.

At the heart of entrepreneurship is innovation. She CEOs who are innovative are always looking for new and better ways to do things. They are not afraid to take risks and try something new, even if it means stepping outside their comfort zone. They are constantly seeking out new ideas and inspiration, and are willing to experiment and iterate until they find a solution that works.

Another key aspect of the entrepreneurial spirit is a willingness to take risks. She CEOs who are willing to take risks understand that failure is part of the process, and that taking risks is necessary in order to achieve success. They are not afraid to fail, and they know that every failure is an opportunity to learn and grow.

Finally, successful She CEOs have a strong desire to learn and grow. They are always seeking out new knowledge and skills, and are willing to invest time and resources into their own personal and professional development. They understand that growth is a process, and that it requires hard work and dedication.

Some examples of successful She CEOs who embody the entrepreneurial spirit include Sara Blakely, the founder of Spanx, who started her business with just $5,000 and a bold idea; Oprah Winfrey, who overcame a difficult childhood to become one of the most successful media moguls of all time; and Arianna Huffington, who launched The Huffington Post and revolutionized the world of online media.

In order to cultivate your own entrepreneurial spirit, it is important to adopt a growth mindset and a willingness to take risks. You should also make a habit of seeking out new ideas and inspiration, whether through reading, attending conferences and events, or networking with other entrepreneurs.

Another important aspect of the entrepreneurial spirit is a willingness to invest in yourself and your business. This means taking the time to develop your skills and knowledge, and investing in resources that can help you grow your business, such as software, equipment, or a mentor or coach.

The entrepreneurial spirit is a key characteristic of successful She CEOs. By adopting a growth mindset, taking risks, seeking out new ideas and investing in yourself, you can cultivate your own entrepreneurial spirit and achieve success in your business.

> *"Entrepreneurship is living a few years of your life like most people won't so you can spend the rest of your life like most people can't."* – Anonymous

Embodying the Traits of Successful Women in Business: A Guide for She CEOs

As we come to the end of Chapter 3, it's clear that successful women in business possess a unique combination of skills and characteristics that enable them to thrive. From leadership skills and management styles to resilience and determination, creativity and innovation, networking and collaboration, passion and purpose, emotional intelligence, flexibility and adaptability, financial acumen, and entrepreneurial spirit, these traits have all been shown to contribute to the success of women in business.

While there is no one-size-fits-all formula for success, it's clear that these characteristics are essential for any woman looking to thrive as a She CEO. By honing these skills and focusing on personal growth, women can become better leaders, innovators, collaborators, and decision-makers.

It's also important to remember that success is not just about achieving financial or professional goals, but also about finding fulfillment and satisfaction in our work and personal lives. Women who are able to balance their professional and personal responsibilities, maintain a strong support system, and prioritize their own well-being are more likely to achieve long-term success and happiness.

As we move forward in our own journeys as She CEOs, let's remember to cultivate these characteristics, embrace our unique strengths, and stay true to our passions and purposes. With dedication, perseverance, and a willingness to adapt and evolve, we can overcome any challenge and achieve our goals as successful women in business.

As Anne Sweeney once said, *"Define success on your own terms, achieve it by your own rules, and build a life you're proud to live."*

In Chapter 3 of The She CEO Survival Guide, we discussed the characteristics of successful women in business, including leadership skills, resilience, creativity, networking, passion, emotional intelligence, flexibility, financial acumen, and entrepreneurial spirit. Now, we invite you to reflect on your own definition of success and how these characteristics can help you achieve it.

Ask yourself the following thought-provoking questions to gain insight and inspiration on your journey as a She CEO.

❖ What does success mean to you, personally and professionally?

❖ How can you align your personal values and mission with your business goals to achieve success on your own terms?

❖ What characteristics and skills do you possess that contribute to your success as a She CEO?

❖ How can you continue to develop and improve these characteristics and skills to achieve even greater success?

❖ In what ways do you actively cultivate a sense of purpose and mission in your business and personal life?

❖ How can you encourage and support other women in business to define and achieve success on their own terms?

❖ What steps can you take to prioritize your well-being and maintain a healthy work-life balance while pursuing your goals as a She CEO?

CHAPTER 4

Strategies for Thriving as a She CEO

"I love to see a young girl go out and grab the world by the lapels. Life's a bitch. You've got to go out and kick ass." - Maya Angelou

As a She CEO, thriving in your career is about more than just achieving success. It's about overcoming challenges, adapting to change, and maintaining a resilient mindset. This chapter will explore strategies for not only overcoming obstacles but also thriving as a leader. We'll cover a range of topics, including building a strong personal and professional network, developing a growth mindset, managing change, and finding work-life balance. By implementing these strategies, She CEOs can navigate the ever-changing business world and achieve long-term success.

Building A Strong Personal & Professional Network

As a She CEO, building a strong personal and professional network is essential to overcoming challenges and achieving success. A strong network can provide valuable resources, support, and opportunities that can help propel your business forward. In this section, we will explore some strategies for building a strong personal and professional network, including examples from successful female CEOs.

One effective strategy for building a strong network is to attend industry events and conferences. These events provide opportunities to meet other professionals in your field, learn from industry experts, and stay up-to-date on the latest trends and developments. Female CEOs like Sheryl Sandberg, COO of Facebook, and Ginni Rometty, former CEO of IBM, have emphasized the importance of attending industry events and conferences.

Sandberg has said, "If you're offered a seat on a rocket ship, you don't ask what seat. You just get on."

She encourages women to take advantage of every opportunity to attend industry events and to not be afraid to speak up and ask questions. Similarly, Rometty has said, "Be bold. Don't be afraid to be different. Don't be afraid to take risks. Be willing to put yourself out there."

Another strategy for building a strong network is to join professional organizations and associations. These groups provide opportunities to connect with like-minded professionals and gain access to valuable resources and information. For example, Susan Wojcicki, CEO of YouTube, is a member of the National Academy of Engineering and the Yale University Council.

Wojcicki has said, "I joined the National Academy of Engineering because I wanted to be part of a group that was focused on innovation and engineering. Being part of this group has allowed me to connect with other like-minded professionals and learn from their experiences." She also recommends that female entrepreneurs join local business organizations and chambers of commerce to build relationships with other professionals in their communities.

In addition to attending industry events and joining professional organizations, social media can also be a valuable tool for building a strong network. Platforms like LinkedIn and Twitter provide opportunities to connect with other professionals, share content, and engage in industry discussions.

Female CEOs like Arianna Huffington, founder of Thrive Global, and Reshma Saujani, founder of Girls Who Code, have emphasized the importance of using social media to build a network.

Huffington has said, "Social media is a great tool for building relationships and staying connected with people. It allows you to share your thoughts and ideas with a wider audience and connect with people who are interested in what you have to say." Saujani has also emphasized the importance of using social media to build a network, saying, "Social media is a powerful tool for networking and building relationships. It allows you to connect with people from all over the world and build your brand."

Finally, it's important to remember that building a strong network is not just about connecting with other professionals. It's also about building meaningful relationships with family, friends, and mentors. Female CEOs like Oprah Winfrey, founder of OWN, and Sara Blakely, founder of Spanx, have emphasized the importance of building relationships outside of work.

Winfrey has said, "The biggest mistake I've made is not building enough relationships outside of work. I've learned that you can't do it all alone. You need a support system." Blakely has also emphasized the importance of building relationships outside of work, saying, "I'm a big believer in having a strong support system. That includes family, friends, and mentors who can help you navigate the ups and downs of life and business."

Building a strong personal and professional network is essential for She CEOs to overcome challenges and achieve success. Strategies like attending industry events, joining professional organizations, using social media, reaching out to mentors and sponsors, and seeking out collaboration opportunities can all help

She CEOs expand their network and build meaningful connections.

By following the examples of successful female CEOs and entrepreneurs, and utilizing the available resources and tools, She CEOs can create a network that provides them with support, advice, and opportunities for growth.

As Stacy Brown-Philpot, former CEO of TaskRabbit, stated, "Building relationships is the key to success in business. You can't do it alone." Therefore, it is important for She CEOs to prioritize networking and collaboration as a key part of their business strategy.

Ultimately, building a strong personal and professional network is crucial for success in business. As Rosalind Brewer, CEO of Walgreens Boots Alliance, emphasizes, "You can't do it alone. You need a strong network of people who believe in you and are willing to support you." By investing time and effort into building and maintaining relationships with others, women entrepreneurs can expand their knowledge, gain new perspectives, and open up new opportunities for their businesses.

Developing A Strong Leadership Style

Developing a strong leadership style is crucial for any She CEO who wants to succeed in today's business world. It involves creating a vision, setting goals, making decisions, and inspiring others to work together towards a common goal. While there is no one-size-fits-all approach to leadership, there are certain characteristics that many successful leaders share.

One of the most important traits of effective leadership is the ability to communicate clearly and inspire others. This includes being able to articulate a vision for the future and motivate employees to work towards that vision. As business leader Richard Branson once said, "Communication is the most important skill any leader can possess."

It's essential for She CEOs to be able to communicate their goals, values, and expectations to their employees and stakeholders.

Another key aspect of strong leadership is the ability to make decisions and take calculated risks.

As a leader, it's important to be able to weigh the pros and cons of a situation and make tough decisions when necessary. This requires confidence in one's own abilities and the ability to gather and analyze information effectively. She CEOs who can make bold decisions and take calculated risks are often more successful in driving their businesses forward.

In addition to communication and decision-making skills, effective leaders also possess strong emotional intelligence. This means being able to understand and manage one's own emotions and those of others in the workplace. By being empathetic and understanding towards employees, leaders can create a positive and productive work environment. As author and leadership expert Simon Sinek once said, "A leader's job is not to do the work for others, it's to help others figure out how to do it themselves, to get things done, and to succeed beyond what they thought possible."

Finally, a strong leadership style involves being adaptable and willing to learn and grow. In today's rapidly changing business landscape, it's important for leaders to be able to pivot and adjust to new challenges and opportunities. This requires a willingness to learn from mistakes and take feedback from others. As Microsoft CEO Satya Nadella once said, "The most important yardstick of success is the way we treat others – our customers, partners, and colleagues."

In summary, developing a strong leadership style is essential for She CEOs who want to succeed in today's business world. This involves effective communication, decision-making skills, emotional intelligence, and adaptability.

By possessing these traits and continually learning and growing as leaders, She CEOs can inspire their employees and drive their businesses towards success.

Cultivating A Sense of Purpose & Mission

As a She CEO, cultivating a sense of purpose and mission is essential for success. Having a clear purpose and mission can help guide decision-making, inspire employees, and attract customers who share your values. A mission-driven approach can also help build a strong brand and reputation, leading to long-term success and sustainability.

One way to cultivate a sense of purpose and mission is by defining your company's values and goals. This involves reflecting on your own values as a leader and aligning them with the values of your company. It also involves defining your company's goals, both short-term and long-term, and creating a plan for achieving them. By having a clear set of values and goals, you can create a sense of purpose for yourself and your employees.

Another way to cultivate a sense of purpose and mission is by communicating your values and goals to your employees and customers. This can involve creating a mission statement, which is a concise statement that communicates your company's values and goals. It can also involve regularly communicating with your employees and customers about your company's progress and how it aligns with your values and goals.

One example of a company that has successfully cultivated a sense of purpose and mission is Patagonia, an outdoor clothing company.

Patagonia's mission statement is "We're in business to save our home planet." This mission statement is reflected in everything the company does, from its sustainable production methods to its advocacy for environmental causes. Patagonia's mission-driven approach has helped the company build a strong brand and reputation, leading to long-term success and a loyal customer base.

Research has shown that having a sense of purpose and mission can have significant benefits for businesses. A study by Deloitte found that purpose-driven companies outperform their peers in terms of revenue growth, profitability, and employee satisfaction. Another study by Imperative and New York University found that purpose-driven employees are more engaged and productive than those who lack a sense of purpose.

As a She CEO, it's important to take a mission-driven approach to leadership and to cultivate a sense of purpose for yourself and your employees. By defining your company's values and goals, communicating them effectively, and aligning your actions with your mission, you can build a strong brand and reputation, attract customers who share your values, and achieve long-term success and sustainability.

Cultivating a sense of purpose and mission is essential for She CEOs who want to build successful and sustainable businesses. Defining your company's values and goals, communicating them effectively, and aligning your actions with your mission can help build a strong brand and reputation and attract customers who share your values. By taking a mission-driven approach to leadership, She CEOs can achieve long-term success and make a positive impact in the world.

To help illustrate this point, we have created a sample mission statement for a hypothetical company.

This mission statement is designed to reflect the values and vision of a company committed to making a positive impact in the world while also achieving success and growth. By examining this mission statement and the thought process behind it, She CEOs can gain insights into how they can craft a mission statement that resonates with their own goals and values.

Here's an example of a mission statement for a company focused on sustainability:

"Our mission is to lead the charge in creating a sustainable future for our planet. Through innovative practices and a commitment to ethical business, we strive to reduce our environmental impact and support the communities in which we operate. By inspiring others to join us in our mission, we aim to create a movement towards a greener, more equitable world."

This mission statement highlights the company's focus on sustainability and ethical business practices, as well as their goal to inspire others to join their mission.

Embracing Innovation and Creativity

Innovation and creativity are essential for success in any business, and this is particularly true for She CEOs who are leading their companies in today's rapidly changing and competitive business world. Embracing innovation and creativity can help She CEOs develop new products and services, improve operations, and stay ahead of the competition. In this section, we will explore the importance of innovation and creativity in business and provide examples of how other female CEOs have successfully implemented innovative and creative strategies to achieve success.

Research has shown that companies that prioritize innovation and creativity are more likely to achieve long-term success. A study by McKinsey & Company found that companies that prioritize innovation generate higher revenue growth and shareholder returns than companies that do not prioritize innovation. Additionally, a survey by PwC found that 61% of CEOs believe that innovation is a key driver of their company's success.

She CEOs can encourage innovation and creativity within their companies by creating a culture that values and rewards new ideas, experimentation, and risk-taking. This can include providing opportunities for employees to brainstorm and collaborate, allocating resources and time for research and development, and fostering a supportive and open-minded workplace culture.

Female CEOs have demonstrated the power of embracing innovation and creativity in their businesses. For example, Sara Blakely, founder of Spanx, revolutionized the hosiery industry by creating a line of slimming undergarments for women.

She initially started the business as a side project while working as a salesperson and used her own savings to fund the venture. Her innovative approach to hosiery quickly caught on, and she built a multimillion-dollar company.

Another example is Katrina Lake, the founder of Stitch Fix, a subscription-based personal styling service. She founded the company in 2011 and has since grown it to a valuation of over $2 billion. Lake attributes the success of her business to her innovative approach to personal styling, which utilizes data and technology to provide personalized clothing recommendations to customers.

Innovation and creativity can also be applied to business operations to improve efficiency and effectiveness. For example, Mary Barra, CEO of General Motors, implemented a new operating model that focuses on collaboration and decision-making efficiency. This approach has led to significant cost savings and improved productivity for the company.

Embracing innovation and creativity is essential for She CEOs to achieve success in today's competitive business world. By creating a culture that values new ideas, experimentation, and risk-taking, She CEOs can encourage innovation and drive growth within their companies. The success stories of female CEOs like Sara Blakely, Katrina Lake, and Mary Barra demonstrate the power of innovation and creativity in business.

Managing Change and Adapting to New Challenges

In today's fast-paced business environment, it is essential for She CEOs to be able to manage change and adapt to new challenges. Organizations that are not able to adapt to changes in the market, technology, and customer demands risk becoming irrelevant or obsolete. Therefore, it is critical for She CEOs to develop the ability to manage change and adapt to new challenges.

One of the key factors in managing change and adapting to new challenges is having a flexible mindset. She CEOs need to be open to new ideas, willing to take risks, and able to pivot when necessary. This flexibility can help She CEOs to identify new opportunities and respond quickly to changes in the market.

Another important aspect of managing change and adapting to new challenges is having a strong team. She CEOs need to build a team of employees who are also flexible and willing to adapt to change. It is essential for She CEOs to communicate with their team regularly, providing them with clear goals and objectives, and involving them in decision-making processes.

In addition, She CEOs can implement strategies such as scenario planning to prepare for potential changes and disruptions. Scenario planning involves identifying different potential scenarios and developing plans to respond to each one. This can help She CEOs to be better prepared for unexpected changes.

Furthermore, She CEOs should also embrace technology and innovation. Technology can help organizations to be more efficient and productive, as well as to better respond to changes in the market. She CEOs should stay up-to-date with the latest technological advancements and look for ways to incorporate them into their business.

Moreover, She CEOs can also seek out mentorship and guidance from experienced business leaders. This can provide valuable insights and advice on managing change and adapting to new challenges. Additionally, joining industry associations and attending relevant events can also help She CEOs to stay informed about new developments in their field and connect with other business leaders.

Finally, it is crucial for She CEOs to maintain a positive and proactive mindset when faced with challenges and changes. By viewing challenges as opportunities and maintaining a growth mindset, She CEOs can more effectively manage change and adapt to new challenges.

In summary, managing change and adapting to new challenges is essential for She CEOs to succeed in today's business world. Strategies such as having a flexible mindset, building a strong team, implementing scenario planning, embracing technology and innovation, seeking mentorship and guidance, and maintaining a positive mindset can all help She CEOs to effectively manage change and adapt to new challenges.

Congratulations, you've made it to the end of Chapter 4: Strategies for Thriving as a She CEO.

We've covered a lot of ground in this chapter, from building a strong personal and professional network to developing a growth mindset, accessing capital and funding, and much more.

But we're not done yet!

Before you go, we want to leave you with some thought-provoking questions that will help you reflect on what you've learned and take action to implement these strategies in your own life and business.

So take a moment to grab a pen and paper, and let's dive in.

❖ How can you build a stronger personal and professional network to support your growth as a She CEO?

❖ What steps can you take to develop a growth mindset and build confidence in yourself and your abilities?

❖ How can you balance your work and personal responsibilities to avoid burnout and maintain your well-being?

❖ What strategies can you use to access capital and funding to grow your business?

❖ How can you stay inspired and motivated by cultivating a sense of purpose and mission in your work?

❖ What are some ways you can embrace innovation and creativity to stay ahead of the competition and adapt to changing markets?

❖ What specific action steps can you take to thrive as a She CEO and achieve the success you desire?

CHAPTER 5

Case Studies
and Success Stories

As a She CEO, it can be challenging to navigate the business world and achieve success. That's why it's essential to learn from the experiences of others who have been in your shoes. In this chapter, we will explore case studies and success stories of women who have overcome obstacles and achieved incredible success in their respective fields. These stories can provide inspiration and valuable insights into what it takes to thrive as a female leader in today's business world.

Profiles of Successful Women in Business

Of all the challenges that She CEOs face, few are as daunting as trying to build a successful business in a male-dominated world. However, there are many successful women in business who have shattered the glass ceiling and paved the way for other women to follow in their footsteps. Their stories serve as an inspiration to all women entrepreneurs who are striving to achieve success in their own right.

This section highlights the profiles of successful women in business who have made a significant impact in their respective industries. From tech innovators to fashion icons, these women have overcome numerous obstacles and challenges to build thriving businesses and become leaders in their fields.

Each profile provides a glimpse into the personal and professional journey of these successful women, revealing the unique qualities and characteristics that helped them overcome obstacles, navigate change, and achieve success. Their stories showcase the importance of traits such as resilience, determination, creativity, innovation, and leadership, which are critical for She CEOs looking to succeed in today's business landscape.

By studying the experiences and insights of these successful women in business, She CEOs can gain valuable insights into the strategies and approaches that have helped them overcome challenges and achieve success. From embracing innovation and creativity to developing a strong leadership style, these women have much to teach us about what it takes to thrive in business and overcome obstacles.

The profiles in this section offer a wealth of inspiration, guidance, and practical advice for She CEOs who are looking to build successful businesses and make a positive impact in their communities. Through their stories, these women serve as powerful role models for all women entrepreneurs, reminding us that with determination, hard work, and a commitment to excellence, anything is possible.

Oprah Winfrey

Oprah Winfrey is an American media executive, actress, talk show host, television producer, and philanthropist. She was born in Mississippi in 1954 and grew up in poverty, facing many challenges in her early life, including abuse and trauma.

Despite the obstacles she faced, Winfrey excelled academically and went on to become one of the most successful and influential women in media. In 1986, she launched The Oprah Winfrey Show, which became the highest-rated daytime talk show in American television history. The show ran for 25 seasons and earned Winfrey numerous awards and accolades, including multiple Emmys and a Presidential Medal of Freedom.

Winfrey's success extends beyond her talk show. She is also a successful actress, producer, and media executive. She founded Harpo Productions in 1986, which produces several popular shows, including Dr. Phil, The Dr. Oz Show, and Super Soul Sunday.

In addition, Winfrey launched the Oprah Winfrey Network (OWN) in 2011, which features original programming focused on self-improvement and personal growth.

Winfrey is known for her philanthropic work and has donated millions of dollars to support causes related to education, health, and empowerment of women and girls. She also established the Oprah Winfrey Leadership Academy for Girls in South Africa, which provides educational opportunities for underprivileged girls.

Throughout her career, Winfrey has demonstrated strong leadership skills, a commitment to personal growth and development, and a willingness to use her platform for social and humanitarian causes. She is a role model and inspiration for many women in business and beyond, and her success serves as a testament to the power of perseverance, hard work, and determination.

Sara Blakely

Sara Blakely is an American entrepreneur and the founder of Spanx, a women's undergarment company. Born in Clearwater, Florida, in 1971, Blakely started her career selling fax machines door-to-door before developing her idea for Spanx.

Blakely's inspiration for Spanx came when she was getting ready for a party and couldn't find a suitable undergarment to wear under white pants. She ended up cutting the feet off a pair of control-top pantyhose and realized that she had stumbled upon a product that many women could use.

Blakely invested her life savings of $5,000 in developing her idea and eventually launched Spanx in 2000. The company quickly became a success, with sales of $4 million in the first year alone.

Today, Spanx is a household name and Blakely has been recognized as one of the world's most successful self-made female billionaires.

One of the keys to Blakely's success is her ability to embrace failure and keep moving forward. She has said, "I've missed more than 9,000 shots in my career. I've lost almost 300 games. Twenty-six times I've been trusted to take the game-winning shot and missed. I've failed over and over and over again in my life. And that is why I succeed."

Blakely is also known for her philanthropy and commitment to empowering women. In 2006, she launched the Sara Blakely Foundation, which supports women through education and entrepreneurship. She has also been a vocal advocate for women in the workplace, encouraging companies to promote gender diversity and support working mothers.

Overall, Sara Blakely's success as an entrepreneur is a testament to her resilience, creativity, and commitment to empowering women.

Sheryl Sandberg

Sheryl Sandberg is an American technology executive and author who is best known for her role as the Chief Operating Officer (COO) of Facebook. She was born on August 28, 1969, in Washington, D.C., and went on to earn a degree in economics from Harvard University.

Sandberg began her career in 1991 as a management consultant at McKinsey & Company, where she worked for six years before joining Google in 2001 as the Vice President of Global Online Sales and Operations. She was instrumental in developing Google's advertising business and helped the company become one of the most successful tech companies in history.

In 2008, Sandberg was hired by Facebook as the company's COO, where she played a crucial role in the company's growth and success. She helped Facebook increase its revenue from $56 million in 2008 to $17.9 billion in 2015, and she oversaw the company's transition from a small startup to a global tech giant.

Sandberg is also the author of several books, including the best-selling book "Lean In: Women, Work, and the Will to Lead," which focuses on women in the workplace and encourages women to take leadership roles in their careers. The book was named one of the best books of the year by several publications, including Time, Fortune, and The Economist.

Throughout her career, Sandberg has been a vocal advocate for women in leadership roles and has worked to promote diversity and inclusion in the workplace. She has been recognized for her contributions to the tech industry and for her advocacy work, receiving numerous awards and honors, including being named one of the 100 most influential people in the world by Time magazine in 2013, 2014, and 2015.

Sandberg's success serves as an inspiration to women in the tech industry and beyond, showing that with hard work, dedication, and a commitment to making a difference, anyone can achieve their goals and make a meaningful impact in the world.

Ursula Burns

Ursula Burns is an American businesswoman who is best known for her tenure as the CEO of Xerox Corporation. She is a true trailblazer in the business world, and her story is an inspiration to women everywhere.

Born in a New York City housing project in 1958, Burns was raised by her single mother, who worked as a nurse. Despite facing many challenges, Burns was determined to succeed. She attended Cathedral High School, an all-girls Catholic school in Manhattan, where she was an excellent student. Burns went on to attend the Polytechnic Institute of New York University, where she earned a degree in mechanical engineering.

After graduation, Burns began her career at Xerox as a summer intern in 1980. She quickly climbed the ranks of the company, holding a variety of positions in engineering, product development, and management. In 2009, she was named the CEO of Xerox, becoming the first African American woman to lead a Fortune 500 company.

As CEO, Burns oversaw a major restructuring of the company, which included a shift towards digital products and services. She also championed diversity and inclusion in the workplace, and was named by Forbes as one of the "World's 100 Most Powerful Women" multiple times. In 2016, Burns stepped down as CEO of Xerox, but she continued to serve as the chairwoman of the board until the company was acquired by Fujifilm in 2018.

Throughout her career, Burns has been a vocal advocate for women and minorities in the workplace. She has spoken out about the importance of diversity and inclusion, and has worked to create opportunities for underrepresented groups.

Burns has also served on the board of several prominent organizations, including American Express, Exxon Mobil, and the Massachusetts Institute of Technology.

In addition to her business accomplishments, Burns is also a philanthropist and has given back to her community in many ways. She has served as a trustee for several educational institutions, including the University of Rochester and the New York City Ballet. In 2010, she was appointed by President Obama to lead the White House national program on Science, Technology, Engineering, and Math (STEM) Education.

Burns is a true inspiration to women in business and a powerful example of what can be achieved through hard work, determination, and a commitment to making a difference. Her legacy as a trailblazer will continue to inspire future generations of women to break barriers and achieve their dreams.

Mary Barra

Mary Barra is a successful American businesswoman who currently serves as the Chairman and CEO of General Motors, making her the first female CEO of a major global automaker. Barra has been with GM for over 40 years, working her way up from an entry-level position to the highest leadership role in the company.

Barra became CEO in 2014 and has since been instrumental in transforming GM's business and culture. She has prioritized innovation and technology, leading the company's efforts to develop and produce electric and autonomous vehicles. Under her leadership, GM has also made a commitment to sustainability, aiming to achieve a zero-emissions future.

Barra has been recognized for her leadership and business acumen, being named to Forbes' list of the World's 100 Most Powerful Women multiple times. In addition to her role at GM, Barra serves on the board of directors for several organizations, including the Walt Disney Company and the Detroit Economic Club. Barra's success is a testament to her dedication and hard work, as well as her ability to lead with a clear vision and commitment to innovation and sustainability. She serves as an inspiration and role model for aspiring female leaders in the business world.

Whitney Wolfe Herd

Whitney Wolfe Herd is a successful American entrepreneur and founder of the dating app Bumble. She was born in Salt Lake City, Utah in 1989 and later attended Southern Methodist University in Dallas, Texas. Wolfe Herd began her career in tech by working for Hatch Labs, a startup incubator in New York City, where she was part of the team that developed the dating app, Tinder.

After leaving Tinder due to a lawsuit, Wolfe Herd founded Bumble in 2014, a dating app that empowers women to make the first move. The app has since expanded to include features such as Bumble BFF for platonic friendships and Bumble Bizz for professional networking.

Under Wolfe Herd's leadership, Bumble has become a major player in the tech industry, valued at over $8 billion as of 2021. Wolfe Herd has been recognized for her entrepreneurial success, including being named to the Forbes 30 Under 30 list in 2017 and 2018, and the TIME 100 list in 2018.

Wolfe Herd is also known for her advocacy work, particularly in the area of gender equality. She has spoken out about the need for greater representation of women in tech and has established the Bumble Fund, which invests in early-stage companies founded and led by women of color.

Through her innovative approach to the dating app industry and her commitment to creating more opportunities for women in tech, Whitney Wolfe Herd has become a notable figure in the world of entrepreneurship and a role model for aspiring female business leaders.

Reshma Saujani

Reshma Saujani is an American lawyer and politician who is best known for founding Girls Who Code, a non-profit organization that aims to close the gender gap in technology by inspiring, educating, and equipping young girls with the computing skills they need to pursue careers in the field.

Saujani's journey to becoming a successful entrepreneur began with a failed bid for Congress in 2010. However, this experience inspired her to take action to address the gender gap in technology, and in 2012, she founded Girls Who Code with the goal of teaching one million girls to code by 2020.

Through her work with Girls Who Code, Saujani has become a leading advocate for women in technology, and her organization has had a significant impact on the industry. By 2018, Girls Who Code had reached over 90,000 girls in all 50 US states, and the organization has been recognized by a number of high-profile supporters, including former First Lady Michelle Obama.

In addition to her work with Girls Who Code, Saujani is also a frequent speaker and commentator on issues related to technology, politics, and gender. She has delivered two TED talks, and her writing has been published in a variety of publications, including The New York Times, The Washington Post, and Fortune.

Saujani's story is a testament to the power of perseverance and determination, and her work has had a significant impact on the lives of countless young girls across the United States. Through her leadership and advocacy, Saujani has helped to inspire a new generation of women in technology, and her work will undoubtedly continue to shape the industry for years to come.

Anne Wojcicki

Anne Wojcicki is an American entrepreneur and co-founder and CEO of the personal genomics and biotechnology company 23andMe. Wojcicki was born in San Mateo County, California, in 1973. She graduated from Yale University with a degree in biology in 1996 and went on to work as a healthcare consultant at the investment bank Investor AB. In 2006, she co-founded 23andMe with Linda Avey, a biotech entrepreneur.

Wojcicki's vision was to create a service that could provide people with access to their genetic information in a way that was affordable and easy to understand. 23andMe offers personalized genetic testing services to help people learn about their ancestry, health risks, and carrier status for certain inherited conditions.

Under Wojcicki's leadership, 23andMe has become one of the most successful consumer genomics companies in the world. The company has raised more than $790 million in funding, and its database now includes DNA samples from more than 12 million people. In 2015, the company was valued at $1.1 billion.

Wojcicki has been recognized as one of the most powerful women in business by Forbes, Fortune, and Time. She has also been an outspoken advocate for women in tech and for the importance of genetic testing and personalized medicine.

Ginni Rometty

Ginni Rometty is an American business executive who is widely known for her tenure as the CEO of IBM from 2012 to 2020. She is a prominent figure in the technology industry and is recognized for her leadership skills and contributions to the advancement of technology.

Rometty began her career with IBM in 1981 as a systems engineer, and she worked her way up through the ranks over the years. She held several executive positions at the company, including Senior Vice President and Group Executive for Sales, Marketing, and Strategy. In 2012, Rometty was named the CEO of IBM, becoming the first woman to lead the company.

As CEO, Rometty led IBM through a period of transformation, focusing on the development of artificial intelligence and cloud computing technologies. She also oversaw the acquisition of several companies, including Red Hat Inc. for $34 billion, which was the largest software acquisition in history at the time.

Under Rometty's leadership, IBM also placed a strong emphasis on diversity and inclusion in the workplace. She established new programs and initiatives to support women and underrepresented minorities in technology and encouraged the company's employees to embrace diversity.

Throughout her career, Rometty has received numerous awards and recognitions for her leadership and contributions to the technology industry. In 2014, she was named to Fortune's list of the "50 Most Powerful Women in Business," and she was also listed among Forbes' "World's 100 Most Powerful Women" for several years.

Rometty's career is a testament to the power of strong leadership and a commitment to innovation and diversity. Her accomplishments as CEO of IBM serve as an inspiration for women in business and technology, showing that with hard work and determination, anything is possible.

Reshma Shetty

Reshma Shetty is a successful entrepreneur and scientist in the field of synthetic biology. She co-founded Ginkgo Bioworks, a biotech startup that designs microbes for a variety of applications. Shetty earned her PhD in biological engineering from the Massachusetts Institute of Technology (MIT), where she developed new methods for engineering microbial communities.

Before co-founding Ginkgo Bioworks, Shetty worked as a research fellow at the Wyss Institute for Biologically Inspired Engineering at Harvard University. She also served as a consultant for pharmaceutical and biotech companies.

In 2008, Shetty co-founded Ginkgo Bioworks with several colleagues from MIT. The company's goal is to create new materials and products using engineered microorganisms. Ginkgo Bioworks has developed microbes that can produce fragrances, flavors, and cosmetics ingredients, as well as specialty enzymes for industrial applications.

Under Shetty's leadership, Ginkgo Bioworks has grown rapidly and has raised over $2 billion in funding from investors such as Viking Global Investors and General Atlantic. In 2020, the company went public through a merger with a special purpose acquisition company (SPAC).

Shetty has been recognized for her achievements in both science and business. In 2016, she was named a Young Global Leader by the World Economic Forum. She has also been named to Fortune's 40 under 40 list and MIT Technology Review's Innovators Under 35 list.

Through her work at Ginkgo Bioworks, Shetty has shown that it is possible to combine scientific expertise with business acumen to create a successful startup. Her innovative approach to synthetic biology has the potential to transform a range of industries and create new products that benefit society.

Bozoma Saint John

Bozoma Saint John, also known as Boz, is a marketing executive who has made a significant impact in the tech industry. She was born in Ghana and raised in Colorado and attended Wesleyan University where she graduated with a degree in African American Studies and English.

Boz started her career in advertising, working for agencies such as Arnold Worldwide and Spike Lee's SpikeDDB. She then moved on to become the head of music and entertainment marketing at PepsiCo, where she led innovative campaigns featuring artists like Beyoncé and Nicki Minaj.

In 2016, Boz joined Uber as the Chief Brand Officer, where she was tasked with revamping the company's image and restoring its reputation after a series of scandals. She implemented a new brand strategy and marketing campaign, which helped to improve customer sentiment and brand perception.

Boz has also held executive positions at Apple Music and Endeavor, where she was the Chief Marketing Officer. In 2019, she became the Chief Marketing Officer of entertainment and sports agency, William Morris Endeavor (WME), where she is responsible for the marketing and branding of the agency's clients.

Boz has been recognized for her work and influence in the industry, including being named one of AdWeek's 30 Most Powerful Women in Sports, one of Fast Company's 100 Most

Creative People in Business, and one of Billboard's Women in Music. She is also a sought-after speaker on topics such as branding, leadership, and diversity in the workplace.

In addition to her professional achievements, Boz is also a vocal advocate for diversity and inclusion in the tech industry. She has spoken about the importance of creating more opportunities for underrepresented groups, particularly women and people of color, and has worked to inspire the next generation of leaders through mentorship and community involvement.

Boz's career trajectory and her dedication to championing diversity and inclusion make her a role model for aspiring female entrepreneurs and leaders. Her innovative marketing strategies and leadership style serve as an inspiration to women in the tech industry and beyond.

These women are just a few examples of the many successful women in business who have overcome challenges and achieved remarkable success. Their stories serve as a reminder that with hard work, determination, and a willingness to take risks, anything is possible.

The profiles of successful women in business serve as a source of inspiration and motivation for aspiring She CEOs. These women have demonstrated the importance of passion, persistence, and hard work in achieving success. They have also overcome challenges and barriers, shattered glass ceilings, and paved the way for future generations of women leaders.

Their stories highlight the power of determination, creativity, and innovation, as well as the importance of building a supportive network, embracing change, and staying true to one's values and mission. By learning from their experiences and adopting their strategies, She CEOs can overcome obstacles, seize opportunities, and achieve their goals.

As women continue to break barriers and make strides in the business world, it is important to celebrate and learn from their successes. By highlighting the stories of successful women in business, we can inspire and empower the next generation of women leaders to achieve their dreams and create a more inclusive and equitable future.

While there are many successful women in business who have achieved their goals through hard work and determination, there are also those who have faced significant challenges along the way.

These women serve as examples of what can be accomplished with perseverance, grit, and a willingness to overcome obstacles.

The following case studies highlight some of these remarkable women and their journeys to success.

Malala Yousafzai

Overcoming Oppression and Advocating for Education

Malala Yousafzai is a Pakistani activist for female education who became known for her advocacy work as a young teenager. At the age of 15, she survived an assassination attempt by the Taliban, who were opposed to her education activism.

Following her recovery, Malala continued to advocate for women's education and human rights, becoming the youngest Nobel laureate in history at the age of 17. Her bravery and dedication have inspired millions of people around the world to stand up for their rights and pursue their dreams, despite the challenges they may face.

J.K. Rowling

Overcoming Rejection and Achieving Success As A Writer

Before J.K. Rowling became one of the world's most successful authors, she faced numerous setbacks and rejections. Her first Harry Potter manuscript was rejected by twelve publishers before it was finally accepted, and even then, she was told to get a day job because there was no money in children's books. Despite these challenges, Rowling persisted and eventually achieved incredible success, becoming one of the best-selling authors of all time. Her story serves as a reminder that rejection and failure are a natural part of the path to success, and that persistence and determination are key to achieving one's goals.

Oprah Winfrey

Overcoming Poverty & Discrimination to Become A Media Mogul

Oprah Winfrey's journey to success is well-known and celebrated. Born into poverty in rural Mississippi, she overcame significant obstacles, including abuse and discrimination, to become one of the most successful and influential media figures of all time. Oprah's story demonstrates the power of perseverance, self-belief, and a willingness to work hard in pursuit of one's dreams.

Angela Duckworth

Overcoming Self-Doubt & Achieving Success as a Psychologist

Angela Duckworth is a psychologist and author who is best known for her work on the concept of grit, which she defines as a combination of passion and perseverance in pursuit of long-term goals. However, Duckworth's own journey to success was not without its challenges.

Despite graduating from Harvard and earning a PhD in psychology from the University of Pennsylvania, she struggled with self-doubt and uncertainty about her career path. Through persistence and determination, she eventually found her niche in the field of psychology and became a leading authority on the subject of grit.

Sheryl Sandberg

Overcoming Gender Bias and Becoming Leader in Tech
Sheryl Sandberg is a prominent technology executive and author who has become a leading voice for women in the workplace. Despite facing significant gender bias and discrimination in the tech industry, Sandberg persisted
and became the Chief Operating Officer of Facebook, one of the world's largest and most influential technology companies. Through her work and advocacy, she has helped to inspire and empower countless women to pursue careers in technology and other male-dominated fields.

These case studies demonstrate the power of perseverance, determination, and resilience in the face of challenges and obstacles. Whether it is overcoming oppression, rejection, poverty, self-doubt, or gender bias, these women have shown that it is possible to achieve success and make a difference in the world, no matter what obstacles may stand in the way.

The case studies of women who have overcome specific challenges and achieved success serve as powerful examples of the resilience, determination, and innovation that are required to succeed in business. These women have faced a variety of obstacles, from gender bias and discrimination to personal setbacks and financial struggles, but they have persevered through their challenges and emerged stronger and more successful.

Their stories serve as inspiration and motivation for other women entrepreneurs who may be facing similar obstacles. By sharing their experiences and insights, these women have not only achieved success for themselves but also paved the way for future generations of women to succeed in business.

Women entrepreneurs bring unique perspectives, skills, and strengths to the business world, and it is essential that their contributions are recognized and supported. By learning from the experiences of these successful women, and by supporting and empowering the next generation of women entrepreneurs, we can continue to drive positive change and create a more diverse, inclusive, and successful business world.

CHAPTER 6

Summary of Key Points
& Closing

Welcome to the final chapter of The She CEO Survival Guide! Throughout this book, we've explored the unique challenges faced by women in leadership roles and provided practical strategies for overcoming these challenges and achieving success. In this chapter, we'll summarize the key points discussed in the previous chapters and provide a comprehensive overview of the strategies that can help She CEOs thrive in their businesses. From building a strong network to accessing capital and funding, we'll cover the essential lessons that every She CEO needs to know. So, let's dive in and review the key takeaways from this guide, and how they can be applied to your journey as a successful She CEO.

Throughout this book for She CEOs, we have discussed various strategies and tips for overcoming challenges and achieving success including:

❖ Building a strong personal and professional network is crucial for She CEOs to overcome challenges and access resources. As a She CEO, it's important to build a network of trusted advisors, mentors, peers, and industry experts who can offer guidance, support, and access to resources. Networking events, industry conferences, online communities, and social media platforms are great places to connect with other professionals and build relationships that can benefit your business.

❖ Developing a growth mindset and building confidence can help She CEOs overcome self-doubt and imposter syndrome. As a She CEO, it's important to have a positive mindset that embraces learning and growth. This means recognizing that failure and setbacks are opportunities to learn and improve, and focusing on your strengths and accomplishments to build confidence. Working with a coach or mentor, practicing self-care, and learning to manage stress can also help build confidence and resilience.

❖ Balancing work and personal responsibilities is essential for maintaining well-being and avoiding burnout. As a She CEO, it's important to prioritize self-care and set boundaries between work and personal life. This means delegating tasks, taking breaks when needed, and finding time for hobbies and activities that bring joy and relaxation. Investing in self-care and mental health is essential for staying energized and focused as a leader.

❖ Accessing capital and funding is a significant challenge for many women entrepreneurs, but there are various strategies and resources available. As a She CEO, it's important to explore a range of funding options, including traditional sources like loans and grants, as well as alternative strategies like crowdfunding and microloans. Seeking out organizations and investors that support women-led businesses can also increase your chances of accessing funding.

❖ Cultivating a sense of purpose and mission can inspire and motivate She CEOs, helping them stay focused on their goals. As a She CEO, having a clear purpose and mission for your business can provide direction and motivation for yourself and your team. This means defining your values, setting goals, and communicating a clear vision for your business. Focusing on a sense of purpose can also help you stay resilient and committed during challenging times.

❖ Embracing innovation and creativity can help She CEOs stay ahead of the competition and adapt to changing markets. As a She CEO, it's important to stay informed about industry trends and new technologies, and to be open to new ideas and approaches. Encouraging innovation and creativity among your team can also lead to breakthroughs and competitive advantages.

❖ Managing change and adapting to new challenges is essential for the success of any business, and She CEOs must be prepared to pivot when necessary. As a She CEO, it's important to stay flexible and adaptable in the face of changing markets, customer needs, and business environments. This means being willing to pivot your strategy, experiment with new approaches, and learn from failure. Developing a mindset of agility and resilience can help you navigate challenges and emerge stronger.

❖ Finally, the profiles of successful women in business that we have discussed serve as inspiring examples of what is possible when women pursue their passions and overcome obstacles. As a She CEO, it's important to seek out role models and mentors who can offer guidance and inspiration on your entrepreneurial journey.

❖ Studying the stories of successful women can also help you learn from their experiences and apply their lessons to your own business.

Closing

The She CEO Survival Guide has explored the unique challenges faced by women in leadership roles and provided strategies for overcoming these challenges and achieving success. We have highlighted the importance of building a strong personal and professional network, developing a growth mindset, overcoming imposter syndrome and self-doubt, balancing work and personal responsibilities, accessing capital and funding, embracing innovation and creativity, and cultivating a sense of purpose and mission.

We have also shared inspiring stories of successful women in business who have overcome specific challenges and achieved great success. These women serve as role models and proof that with hard work, determination, and the right strategies, anything is possible.

As we close this book, we want to offer our final words of encouragement and inspiration to all the She CEOs out there.

Remember that you are not alone in facing the challenges that come with leadership. Seek out support from your network, stay true to your values and purpose, and never stop learning and growing.

Keep pushing forward, and always believe in yourself and your abilities. With these strategies and a strong support system, we have no doubt that you will continue to achieve great things and make a positive impact in your organization and beyond.

Thank you for joining us on this journey, and we wish you all the best in your pursuit of success as a She CEO.

Dear Fellow She CEOs,

As we come to the end of The She CEO Survival Guide, I wanted to take a moment to personally congratulate you on your journey thus far. The challenges of being a woman in leadership can often feel overwhelming and isolating, but I hope this book has provided you with valuable strategies and inspiration to help you navigate these challenges and achieve your goals.

I know firsthand the struggles that come with being a She CEO. The doubts, the imposter syndrome, the balancing act of work and personal responsibilities – it can all feel like too much at times. But I also know that with the right support and strategies, we can overcome these challenges and thrive as leaders.

The key to success is in building a strong personal and professional network. Reach out to other She CEOs, build relationships with mentors, and surround yourself with supportive peers who will help lift you up when you need it most. Remember that you are not alone in your struggles and that together, we can achieve anything.

I also encourage you to continue developing a growth mindset, embracing innovation and creativity, and cultivating a sense of purpose and mission. Stay true to your values and keep pushing forward, even when faced with setbacks and obstacles.

As we close this book, I want to offer my heartfelt thanks to each and every one of you for your dedication and hard work as She CEOs.

I hope this guide has provided you with the tools and inspiration you need to continue thriving as leaders and making a positive impact in your organizations and beyond.

With warmest regards,

Nancy Brown

References

"RUTH BADER GINSBURG'S LIFE AND CAREER IN PHOTOS." NBC NEWS, 18 SEPT. 2020, WWW.NBCNEWS.COM/NEWS/US-NEWS/RUTH-BADER-GINSBURG-S-LIFE-CAREER-PHOTOS-N921956.

"OPRAH WINFREY: THE AMERICAN DREAM." ACADEMY OF ACHIEVEMENT, 17 MAY 2021, ACHIEVEMENT.ORG/ACHIEVER/OPRAH-WINFREY/.

"GM CEO MARY BARRA: FROM THE FACTORY FLOOR TO THE CORNER OFFICE." CBS NEWS, 4 JAN. 2016, WWW.CBSNEWS.COM/NEWS/GM-CEO-MARY-BARRA-FROM-THE-FACTORY-FLOOR-TO-THE-CORNER-OFFICE/.

"SPANX FOUNDER SARA BLAKELY'S JOURNEY FROM DOOR-TO-DOOR SALESWOMAN TO BILLIONAIRE." CNBC, 5 NOV. 2019, WWW.CNBC.COM/2019/11/05/SPANX-FOUNDER-SARA-BLAKELYS-JOURNEY-FROM-DOOR-TO-DOOR-SALESWOMAN-TO-BILLIONAIRE.HTML.

MOSS-RACUSIN, C. A., DOVIDIO, J. F., BRESCOLL, V. L., GRAHAM, M. J., & HANDELSMAN, J. (2012). SCIENCE FACULTY'S SUBTLE GENDER BIASES FAVOR MALE STUDENTS. PROCEEDINGS OF THE NATIONAL ACADEMY OF SCIENCES, 109(41), 16474-16479.

HEILMAN, M. E., & OKIMOTO, T. G. (2007). WHY ARE WOMEN PENALIZED FOR SUCCESS AT MALE TASKS?: THE IMPLIED COMMUNALITY DEFICIT. JOURNAL OF APPLIED PSYCHOLOGY, 92(1), 81-92.

CATALYST. (2018). WOMEN CEOS OF THE S&P 500. CATALYST.

LEAN IN. (N.D.). WOMEN IN THE WORKPLACE 2020. LEAN IN.

NOOYI, I. K. (2018). MY LIFE IN FULL: WORK, FAMILY, AND OUR FUTURE. HACHETTE.

NATIONAL WOMEN'S BUSINESS COUNCIL. (2018). "CREDIT DESERTS: UNDERSTANDING THE LANDSCAPE OF WOMEN'S ACCESS TO CREDIT AND CAPITAL."

KANZE, D., HUANG, L., CONLEY, M. A., & HIGGINS, E. T. (2018). "WE ASK MEN TO WIN AND WOMEN NOT TO LOSE: CLOSING THE GENDER GAP IN STARTUP FUNDING." ACADEMY OF MANAGEMENT JOURNAL, 61(2), 586-614.

BRUSH, C. G., DE BRUIN, A., & WELTER, F. (2009). "A GENDER-AWARE FRAMEWORK FOR WOMEN'S ENTREPRENEURSHIP." INTERNATIONAL JOURNAL OF GENDER AND ENTREPRENEURSHIP, 1(1), 8-24.

GOMPERS, P. A., & WANG, X. (2017). "DIVERSITY IN INNOVATION." HARVARD BUSINESS REVIEW, 95(6), 62-69.

ORSER, B., RIDING, A., & MANLEY, K. (2008). "WOMEN ENTREPRENEURS AND FINANCIAL CAPITAL." ENTREPRENEURSHIP THEORY AND PRACTICE, 32(1), 37-64.

MARLOW, S., & MCADAM, M. (2013). "GENDER AND ENTREPRENEURSHIP: ADVANCING DEBATE AND CHALLENGING MYTHS; EXPLORING THE MYSTERY OF THE UNDER-PERFORMING FEMALE ENTREPRENEUR." INTERNATIONAL JOURNAL OF ENTREPRENEURIAL BEHAVIOR & RESEARCH, 19(1), 114-124.

JOLLY, A., & NEFF, D. (2020). THE SIMPLE TRUTH ABOUT THE GENDER PAY GAP (SPRING 2020). AMERICAN ASSOCIATION OF UNIVERSITY WOMEN (AAUW)

"I HAVE IMPOSTER SYNDROME. HERE'S HOW I DEAL WITH IT" BY RESHMA SAUJANI (HARVARD BUSINESS REVIEW, APRIL 2019)

SEGRAN, E. (2017). FEELING LIKE AN IMPOSTOR? YOU CAN ESCAPE THIS CONFIDENCE-SAPPING SYNDROME. FAST COMPANY.

KAY, K., & SHIPMAN, C. (2014). THE CONFIDENCE GAP. THE ATLANTIC. HTTPS://WWW.THEATLANTIC.COM/MAGAZINE/ARCHIVE/2014/05/THE-CONFIDENCE-GAP/359815/

SANDBERG, S. (2013). LEAN IN: WOMEN, WORK, AND THE WILL TO LEAD. KNOPF.

LEBOWITZ, S. (2019, SEPTEMBER 13). THE WORK-LIFE BALANCE OF A FEMALE CEO: AN INTERVIEW WITH TORY BURCH. BUSINESS INSIDER. HTTPS://WWW.BUSINESSINSIDER.COM/TORY-BURCH-WORK-LIFE-BALANCE-CEO-2019-9

WHITMORE, J. (2018, MAY 11). CEO MOMS SHARE THEIR SECRETS TO WORK-LIFE BALANCE. ENTREPRENEUR. *HTTPS://WWW.ENTREPRENEUR.COM/ARTICLE/313640*

MATUSON, R. A. (2017). THE POWER OF NETWORKING FOR WOMEN ENTREPRENEURS. FORBES. RETRIEVED FROM HTTPS://WWW.FORBES.COM/SITES/ROBBYMOOK/2017/03/28/THE-POWER-OF-NETWORKING-FOR-WOMEN-ENTREPRENEURS/?SH=61F784DD775B

SINGH, S. K. (2019). THE IMPORTANCE OF BUILDING A PROFESSIONAL NETWORK. ENTREPRENEUR. RETRIEVED FROM HTTPS://WWW.ENTREPRENEUR.COM/ARTICLE/338393

TJAN, A. K., & GINO, F. (2018). WHY NETWORKING IS A SKILL YOU CAN'T AFFORD TO NEGLECT. HARVARD BUSINESS REVIEW. RETRIEVED FROM HTTPS://HBR.ORG/2018/06/WHY-NETWORKING-IS-A-SKILL-YOU-CANT-AFFORD-TO-NEGLECT

LEIBOWITZ, S. J., & TOLLIVER, C. (2019). THE ROLE OF GENDER IN VENTURE CAPITAL FUNDING: A BIAS REDUCTION FRAMEWORK. JOURNAL OF BUSINESS DIVERSITY, 19(1), 39-52.

BRUSH, C. G., CARTER, N. M., GATEWOOD, E. J., GREENE, P. G., & HART, M. M. (2006). CLEARING THE HURDLES: WOMEN BUILDING HIGH-GROWTH BUSINESSES. PRENTICE HALL.

COLEMAN, S. (2007). WOMEN, BUSINESS ANGELS AND THE UK VENTURE CAPITAL INDUSTRY: SETTING THE RESEARCH AGENDA. INTERNATIONAL SMALL BUSINESS JOURNAL, 25(5), 449-475.

ORSER, B. J., RIDING, A. L., & MANLEY, K. (2006). WOMEN ENTREPRENEURS AND FINANCIAL CAPITAL. ENTREPRENEURSHIP THEORY AND PRACTICE, 30(5), 643-665.

KANZE, D., HUANG, L., CONLEY, M. A., & HIGGINS, E. T. (2018). WE ASK MEN TO WIN & WOMEN NOT TO LOSE: CLOSING THE GENDER GAP IN STARTUP FUNDING. ACADEMY OF MANAGEMENT JOURNAL, 61(2), 586-614.

CARTER, N. M., SIMKINS, B. J., & SIMPSON, W. G. (2003). CORPORATE GOVERNANCE, BOARD DIVERSITY, AND FIRM VALUE. THE FINANCIAL REVIEW, 38(1), 33-53.

HUANG, L., PEARCE, J. L., & MANZ, C. C. (2015). THE DYNAMICS OF PARTICIPATION IN GENDER-SCIENCE STEREOTYPING INTERVENTIONS. JOURNAL OF APPLIED PSYCHOLOGY, 100(5), 1568-1582.

ORSER, B. J., RIDING, A. L., & MANLEY, K. (2014). WOMEN ENTREPRENEURS' GROWTH-ORIENTED PSYCHOLOGICAL CAPITAL. JOURNAL OF SMALL BUSINESS MANAGEMENT, 52(2), 310-328.

PÁEZ, F., SÁNCHEZ-SELLERO, P., & GUTIÉRREZ-TAÑO, D. (2017). CAPITAL STRUCTURE DECISIONS AND BOARD CHARACTERISTICS: EVIDENCE FROM SPANISH SMES. JOURNAL OF BUSINESS RESEARCH, 78, 257-263.

RYNES, S. L., & ROSEN, B. (1995). A FIELD SURVEY OF FACTORS RELATED TO PERCEIVED GENDER DISCRIMINATION IN EMPLOYMENT. SEX ROLES, 32(9/10), 687-702.

ELTING, LIZ. "5 TRAITS OF HIGHLY SUCCESSFUL WOMEN IN BUSINESS." ENTREPRENEUR, 16 AUG. 2017, HTTPS://WWW.ENTREPRENEUR.COM/ARTICLE/298527.

MCKINSEY & COMPANY. "WOMEN IN THE WORKPLACE 2020." MCKINSEY & COMPANY, SEPT. 2020, HTTPS://WWW.MCKINSEY.COM/FEATURED-INSIGHTS/DIVERSITY-AND-INCLUSION/WOMEN-IN-THE-WORKPLACE-2020.

MILLER, JODY. "THE 7 HABITS OF SUCCESSFUL WOMEN IN BUSINESS." FORBES, 16 NOV. 2016, HTTPS://WWW.FORBES.COM/SITES/JODYMILLER/2016/11/16/THE-7-HABITS-OF-SUCCESSFUL-WOMEN-IN-BUSINESS/?SH=4BAF7C1D2B18.

KING, ANNETTE. "WHY ADAPTABILITY IS KEY TO SUCCESS IN BUSINESS." FORBES, 4 MAR. 2021, HTTPS://WWW.FORBES.COM/SITES/ANNETTEKING/2021/03/04/WHY-ADAPTABILITY-IS-KEY-TO-SUCCESS-IN-BUSINESS/?SH=62DE3D3D3F2C.

GOLEMAN, D. (1998). WHAT MAKES A LEADER? HARVARD BUSINESS REVIEW. HTTPS://HBR.ORG/2004/01/WHAT-MAKES-A-LEADER-2

MINSHEW, K. (2016). 5 QUALITIES OF SUCCESSFUL LEADERS. FORBES. HTTPS://WWW.FORBES.COM/SITES/KATHRYNDILL/2016/02/08/5-QUALITIES-OF-SUCCESSFUL-LEADERS/?SH=5EC5D5C16F5D

PETERSON INSTITUTE FOR INTERNATIONAL ECONOMICS. (2016). IS GENDER DIVERSITY PROFITABLE? EVIDENCE FROM A GLOBAL SURVEY. HTTPS://WWW.PIIE.COM/SYSTEM/FILES/DOCUMENTS/WP16-3.PDF

BERTRAND, M., & SCHOAR, A. (2017). THE GENDER GAP IN STARTUP SUCCESS AND FUNDING. NATIONAL BUREAU OF ECONOMIC RESEARCH. *HTTPS://WWW.NBER.ORG/PAPERS/W23292*

CARDON, M. S., FOO, M. D., SHEPHERD, D., & WIKLUND, J. (2012). EXPLORING THE HEART: ENTREPRENEURIAL EMOTION IS A HOT TOPIC. ENTREPRENEURSHIP THEORY AND PRACTICE, 36(1), 1-10.

CENTRE FOR ENTREPRENEURS. (2015). ENTREPRENEURIAL DETERMINANTS. RETRIEVED FROM HTTPS://CENTREFORENTREPRENEURS.ORG/WP-CONTENT/UPLOADS/2015/08/ENTREPRENEURIAL-DETERMINANTS-AUGUST-2015.PDF

FORBES. (2016). SARA BLAKELY. RETRIEVED FROM HTTPS://WWW.FORBES.COM/PROFILE/SARA-BLAKELY/

HYMAN, J.

LI, J. J., & WU, C. (2019). THE IMPACT OF NETWORKING INTENSITY AND FOUNDER EXPERIENCE ON FIRM INNOVATION: EVIDENCE FROM CHINESE HIGH-TECH FIRMS. ASIA PACIFIC JOURNAL OF MANAGEMENT, 36(2), 405-429. DOI: 10.1007/S10490-018-9546-5

MCADAM, M., & HAZLETT, S. (2011). INTELLECTUAL CAPITAL AND BUSINESS PERFORMANCE IN THE UK FINANCIAL SERVICES SECTOR. JOURNAL OF INTELLECTUAL CAPITAL, 12(4), 537-557. DOI: 10.1108/14691931111174994

AHUJA, G. (2000). COLLABORATION NETWORKS, STRUCTURAL HOLES, AND INNOVATION: A LONGITUDINAL STUDY. ADMINISTRATIVE SCIENCE QUARTERLY, 45(3), 425-455. DOI: 10.2307/2667105

WEST, M. A. (2002). SPARKLING FOUNTAINS OR STAGNANT PONDS: AN INTEGRATIVE MODEL OF CREATIVITY AND INNOVATION IMPLEMENTATION IN WORK GROUPS. APPLIED PSYCHOLOGY, 51(3), 355-387. DOI: 10.1111/1464-0597.00951

SERRAT, O. (2017). NETWORKED GOVERNANCE. IN KNOWLEDGE SOLUTIONS: TOOLS, METHODS, AND APPROACHES TO DRIVE ORGANIZATIONAL PERFORMANCE (PP. 335-343). SPRINGER SINGAPORE. DOI: 10.1007/978-981-10-0983-9_42

GUPTE, M. (2019, JUNE 3). THE IMPORTANCE OF NETWORKING FOR ENTREPRENEURS. ENTREPRENEUR. RETRIEVED FROM HTTPS://WWW.ENTREPRENEUR.COM/ARTICLE/334161

GRESHAM, D. G. (2016). COLLABORATION IN ORGANIZATIONS: A REVIEW OF THE LITERATURE. JOURNAL OF LEADERSHIP, ACCOUNTABILITY AND ETHICS, 13(2), 126-137. DOI: 10.1108/JLAE-02-2015-0008

HURST, D. K. (2017). THE POWER OF COLLABORATION: THE INFLUENCE OF COLLABORATION ON TEAM CREATIVITY AND INNOVATION. INTERNATIONAL JOURNAL OF BUSINESS AND SOCIAL SCIENCE, 8(10), 77-84.

UZZI, B., & SPIRO, J. (2005). COLLABORATION AND CREATIVITY: THE SMALL WORLD PROBLEM. AMERICAN JOURNAL OF SOCIOLOGY, 111(2), 447-504. DOI: 10.1086/432782

ELY, R. J., & MEYERSON, D. E. (2000). THEORIES OF GENDER IN ORGANIZATIONS: A NEW APPROACH TO ORGANIZATIONAL ANALYSIS AND CHANGE. RESEARCH IN ORGANIZATIONAL BEHAVIOR, 22, 103-151. DOI: 10.1016/S0191-3085(00)22004-6

O'NEIL, D. (2018). THE IMPORTANCE OF PASSION IN LEADERSHIP. FORBES. HTTPS://WWW.FORBES.COM/SITES/FORBESCOACHESCOUNCIL/2018/03/01/THE-IMPORTANCE-OF-PASSION-IN-LEADERSHIP/?SH=4B1D8F184C58

LLOPIS, G. (2014). THE IMPORTANCE OF LEADING WITH PURPOSE. FORBES. HTTPS://WWW.FORBES.COM/SITES/GLENNLLOPIS/2014/06/16/THE-IMPORTANCE-OF-LEADING-WITH-PURPOSE/?SH=324C029E4245

RODDICK, A. (2019). THE IMPORTANCE OF PURPOSE-DRIVEN LEADERSHIP. INC. HTTPS://WWW.INC.COM/ADAM-ROBINSON/THE-IMPORTANCE-OF-PURPOSE-DRIVEN-LEADERSHIP.HTML

SCHWARTZ, T. (2019). WHY PURPOSE IS IMPORTANT TO BUSINESS SUCCESS. HARVARD BUSINESS REVIEW. HTTPS://HBR.ORG/2019/05/WHY-PURPOSE-IS-IMPORTANT-TO-BUSINESS-SUCCESS

BAILEY, L. (2019). THE POWER OF PURPOSE-DRIVEN LEADERSHIP. ENTREPRENEUR. HTTPS://WWW.ENTREPRENEUR.COM/ARTICLE/340406

ROSMARIN, R. (2020). THE POWER OF PURPOSE: HOW GREAT COMPANIES DEFINE THEIR PURPOSE TO DRIVE SUCCESS. FORBES. HTTPS://WWW.FORBES.COM/SITES/ROBERTROSMARIN/2020/06/25/THE-POWER-OF-PURPOSE-HOW-GREAT-COMPANIES-DEFINE-THEIR-PURPOSE-TO-DRIVE-SUCCESS/?SH=71F344E94F24

GOUDREAU, J. (2017). THE POWER OF PURPOSE-DRIVEN COMPANIES. FORBES. HTTPS://WWW.FORBES.COM/SITES/JENNAGOUDREAU/2017/05/31/THE-POWER-OF-PURPOSE-DRIVEN-COMPANIES/?SH=447E6A2F6C1D

DWECK, C. (2017). MINDSET: CHANGING THE WAY YOU THINK TO FULFIL YOUR POTENTIAL. RANDOM HOUSE.

PINK, D. (2009). DRIVE: THE SURPRISING TRUTH ABOUT WHAT MOTIVATES US. PENGUIN.

CSIKSZENTMIHALYI, M. (1996). CREATIVITY: FLOW AND THE PSYCHOLOGY OF DISCOVERY AND INVENTION. HARPER COLLINS.

CHIU, C. (2021). HOW TO NETWORK AS A WOMAN ENTREPRENEUR. FORBES. RETRIEVED FROM HTTPS://WWW.FORBES.COM/SITES/CHRISTINECHIU/2021/03/08/HOW-TO-NETWORK-AS-A-WOMAN-ENTREPRENEUR/?SH=18B04962687B

MENON, V. (2019). HOW TO BUILD A POWERFUL PROFESSIONAL NETWORK. BBC. RETRIEVED FROM HTTPS://WWW.BBC.COM/WORKLIFE/ARTICLE/20190212-HOW-TO-BUILD-A-POWERFUL-PROFESSIONAL-NETWORK

MURRAY, R. (2020). 5 TIPS FOR WOMEN ON HOW TO BUILD A STRONG PROFESSIONAL NETWORK. WOMEN'S BUSINESS ENTERPRISE NATIONAL COUNCIL. RETRIEVED FROM HTTPS://WWW.WBENC.ORG/BLOG-POSTS/2020/8/26/5-TIPS-FOR-WOMEN-ON-HOW-TO-BUILD-A-STRONG-PROFESSIONAL-NETWORK

NATIONAL ASSOCIATION OF WOMEN BUSINESS OWNERS. (N.D.). ABOUT US. RETRIEVED FROM HTTPS://WWW.NAWBO.ORG/ABOUT-US

NATIONAL ASSOCIATION OF FEMALE EXECUTIVES. (N.D.). ABOUT NAFE. RETRIEVED FROM HTTPS://NAFE.COM/ABOUT-NAFE

WOMEN IN BUSINESS. (N.D.). ABOUT WIB. RETRIEVED FROM HTTPS://WWW.WOMENINBUSINESSNI.COM/ABOUT-US.ASPX

FORBES. (2018, MAY 22). TORY BURCH: SURROUND YOURSELF WITH PEOPLE WHO INSPIRE YOU. RETRIEVED FROM HTTPS://WWW.FORBES.COM/SITES/MOIRAFORBES/2018/05/22/TORY-BURCH-SURROUND-YOURSELF-WITH-PEOPLE-WHO-INSPIRE-YOU/?SH=181D505A3A22

FORBES. (2016, MAY 26). SPANX FOUNDER SARA BLAKELY: EMBRACE FAILURE AND KEEP TRYING. RETRIEVED FROM HTTPS://WWW.FORBES.COM/SITES/DANSCHAWBEL/2016/05/26/SPANX-FOUNDER-SARA-BLAKELY-EMBRACE-FAILURE-AND-KEEP-TRYING/?SH=7F4D00E6274F

THRIVE GLOBAL. (2021, JANUARY 21). VIPKID FOUNDER CINDY MI: "TAKING CARE OF YOUR OWN MENTAL AND PHYSICAL HEALTH IS IMPORTANT". RETRIEVED FROM HTTPS://THRIVEGLOBAL.COM/STORIES/VIPKID-FOUNDER-CINDY-MI-TAKING-CARE-OF-YOUR-OWN-MENTAL-AND-PHYSICAL-HEALTH-IS-IMPORTANT/

GRANT, A. M., & PATERSON, T. A. (2011). THE BENEFITS OF BEING PRESENT: MINDFULNESS AND ITS ROLE IN PSYCHOLOGICAL WELL-BEING. JOURNAL OF PERSONALITY AND SOCIAL PSYCHOLOGY, 84(4), 822-848.

QUINN, R. E. (2016). THE PARADOXICAL NATURE OF CHANGE. IN THE SAGE HANDBOOK OF PROCESS ORGANIZATION STUDIES (PP. 53-67). SAGE PUBLICATIONS LTD.

WONG, E. (2019). WHY ADAPTABILITY IS THE MOST IMPORTANT SKILL YOU NEED IN THE WORKPLACE. CNBC. RETRIEVED FROM HTTPS://WWW.CNBC.COM/2019/06/27/WHY-ADAPTABILITY-IS-THE-MOST-IMPORTANT-SKILL-YOU-NEED-IN-THE-WORKPLACE.HTML

COUTU, D. L. (2002). HOW RESILIENCE WORKS. HARVARD BUSINESS REVIEW, 80(5), 46-55.

MCKINSEY & COMPANY. (2020). RESPONDING TO CORONAVIRUS: THE MINIMUM VIABLE NERVE CENTER. RETRIEVED FROM *HTTPS://WWW.MCKINSEY.COM/BUSINESS-FUNCTIONS/RISK/OUR-INSIGHTS/RESPONDING-TO-CORONAVIRUS-THE-MINIMUM-VIABLE-NERVE-CENTER*

COX, T. (1994). CULTURAL DIVERSITY IN ORGANIZATIONS: THEORY, RESEARCH, AND PRACTICE. SAN FRANCISCO, CA: BERRETT-KOEHLER PUBLISHERS.

DAVIDSON, M. N., & COOPER, C. L. (1992). SHATTERING THE GLASS CEILING: THE WOMAN MANAGER. NEW YORK, NY: PAUL CHAPMAN PUBLISHING LTD.

HERRING, C. (2009). DOES DIVERSITY PAY? RACE, GENDER, AND THE BUSINESS CASE FOR DIVERSITY. AMERICAN SOCIOLOGICAL REVIEW, 74(2), 208-224.

HUNT, V., LAYTON, D., & PRINCE, S. (2015). DIVERSITY MATTERS. MCKINSEY & COMPANY.

JACKSON, S. E., & RUDERMAN, M. N. (1999). DIVERSITY IN WORK TEAMS: RESEARCH PARADIGMS FOR A CHANGING WORKPLACE. WASHINGTON, DC: AMERICAN PSYCHOLOGICAL ASSOCIATION.

KOCHAN, T., BEZRUKOVA, K., ELY, R., JACKSON, S., JOSHI, A., JEHN, K., ... & THOMAS, D. (2003). THE EFFECTS OF DIVERSITY ON BUSINESS PERFORMANCE: REPORT OF THE DIVERSITY RESEARCH NETWORK. HUMAN RESOURCE MANAGEMENT, 42(1), 3-21.

THOMAS, D. A. (1990). THE IMPACT OF RACE ON MANAGERS' EXPERIENCES OF DEVELOPMENTAL RELATIONSHIPS (MENTORING AND SPONSORSHIP) IN ORGANIZATIONS. JOURNAL OF ORGANIZATIONAL BEHAVIOR, 11(6), 479-492.

TRIANA, M. D. C., GARCÍA, M. A. F., & COLELLA, A. (2014). MANAGING DIVERSITY IN WORK TEAMS: A COMPARATIVE ANALYSIS OF DIFFERENT DIVERSITY TRAINING PROGRAMS. JOURNAL OF BUSINESS AND PSYCHOLOGY, 29(2), 311-327.

BRANSON, R. (2012). LIKE A VIRGIN: SECRETS THEY WON'T TEACH YOU AT BUSINESS SCHOOL. PENGUIN UK.

SINEK, S. (2014). LEADERS EAT LAST: WHY SOME TEAMS PULL TOGETHER AND OTHERS DON'T. PENGUIN UK.

NADELLA, S. (2017). HIT REFRESH: THE QUEST TO REDISCOVER MICROSOFT'S SOUL AND IMAGINE A BETTER FUTURE FOR EVERYONE. HARPERCOLLINS.

DELOITTE. (2019). PURPOSE-DRIVEN LEADERSHIP: WHAT IT IS, WHY IT MATTERS, AND HOW IT CAN TRANSFORM YOUR ORGANIZATION. RETRIEVED FROM HTTPS://WWW2.DELOITTE.COM/US/EN/PAGES/ABOUT-DELOITTE/ARTICLES/PURPOSE-DRIVEN-LEADERSHIP.HTML

IMPERATIVE & NEW YORK UNIVERSITY. (2016). PURPOSE AT WORK. RETRIEVED FROM HTTPS://WWW.IMPERATIVE.COM/WP-CONTENT/UPLOADS/2016/03/PURPOSE-WORK-RESEARCH-REPORT-2016.PDF

AMABILE, T. M. (1988). A MODEL OF CREATIVITY AND INNOVATION IN ORGANIZATIONS. RESEARCH IN ORGANIZATIONAL BEHAVIOR, 10, 123-167.

HENNESSEY, B. A., & AMABILE, T. M. (2010). CREATIVITY. ANNUAL REVIEW OF PSYCHOLOGY, 61, 569-598.

MARTIN, R. L. (2013). THE INNOVATION CATALYSTS. HARVARD BUSINESS REVIEW, 91(6), 78-84.

WEST, M. A., & FARR, J. L. (1990). INNOVATION AND CREATIVITY AT WORK: PSYCHOLOGICAL AND ORGANIZATIONAL STRATEGIES. WILEY.

WOODMAN, R. W., SAWYER, J. E., & GRIFFIN, R. W. (1993). TOWARD A THEORY OF ORGANIZATIONAL CREATIVITY. ACADEMY OF MANAGEMENT REVIEW, 18(2), 293-321.

ANDERSON, P., & JOHNSON, L. (1997). SYSTEMS THINKING BASICS: FROM CONCEPTS TO CAUSAL LOOPS. PEGASUS COMMUNICATIONS.

CHRISTENSEN, C. M. (1997). THE INNOVATOR'S DILEMMA: WHEN NEW TECHNOLOGIES CAUSE GREAT FIRMS TO FAIL. HARVARD BUSINESS REVIEW PRESS.

COLLINS, J. (2001). GOOD TO GREAT: WHY SOME COMPANIES MAKE THE LEAP AND OTHERS DON'T. HARPERBUSINESS.

KOTTER, J. P. (1996). LEADING CHANGE. HARVARD BUSINESS REVIEW PRESS.

MARTIN, R. (2007). THE OPPOSABLE MIND: HOW SUCCESSFUL LEADERS WIN THROUGH INTEGRATIVE THINKING. HARVARD BUSINESS REVIEW PRESS.

TUSHMAN, M. L., & O'REILLY, C. A. (1997). WINNING THROUGH INNOVATION: A PRACTICAL GUIDE TO LEADING ORGANIZATIONAL CHANGE AND RENEWAL. HARVARD BUSINESS PRESS.

THE DIVERSITY, EQUITY & INCLUSION IMPERATIVE: GOING BEYOND GOOD INTENTIONS TO MAKE PROGRESS - HARVARD BUSINESS REVIEW

THE CORPORATE DIVERSITY AND INCLUSION OFFICER: A C-LEVEL ROLE - FORBES

DIVERSITY, EQUITY AND INCLUSION (DEI) FOR BUSINESSES - NATIONAL LGBT CHAMBER OF COMMERCE

CRACE, K. (2021). CONFLICT RESOLUTION. [ONLINE] VPSTUDENTAFFAIRS.WVU.EDU. AVAILABLE AT: HTTPS://STUDENTAFFAIRS.WVU.EDU/ABOUT-US/MEET-THE-VP-FOR-STUDENT-LIFE/CONFLICT-RESOLUTION

AL-HUSAN, F. A. (2019). KNOWLEDGE MANAGEMENT PRACTICES AND ORGANIZATIONAL INNOVATION: THE MEDIATING ROLE OF ORGANIZATIONAL LEARNING CAPABILITY. JOURNAL OF INNOVATION & KNOWLEDGE, 4(2), 85-94.

HOSSAIN, M. A. (2017). EXPLORING THE FACTORS THAT INFLUENCE KNOWLEDGE SHARING BEHAVIOR AMONG EMPLOYEES IN THE E-COMMERCE INDUSTRY. JOURNAL OF KNOWLEDGE MANAGEMENT, 21(1), 136-155.

SARMIENTO, E. (2018). DIGITAL TRANSFORMATION IN THE FASHION INDUSTRY: A CASE STUDY OF DIANE VON FURSTENBERG. JOURNAL OF BUSINESS RESEARCH, 91, 257-264.

ALTAI, A. (2020). SELF-CARE IS NOT A LUXURY, IT'S A NON-NEGOTIABLE. FORBES. RETRIEVED FROM HTTPS://WWW.FORBES.COM/SITES/AMINATAI/2020/02/18/SELF-CARE-IS-NOT-A-LUXURY-ITS-A-NON-NEGOTIABLE/?SH=5FD295D55DD1

NELSON, A. (2018). BUILDING A GREAT TEAM: AMY NELSON, CEO AND FOUNDER OF THE RIVETER. HUFFPOST. RETRIEVED FROM HTTPS://WWW.HUFFPOST.COM/ENTRY/BUILDING-A-GREAT-TEAM-AMY_B_5A9E7918E4B0D4F5B66A334A

TYFTING, M. (2019). SHE CEO: MARILYN TYFTING, CIO AND CPO OF TELUS INTERNATIONAL. WOMEN IN TECHNOLOGY WORLD SERIES. RETRIEVED FROM HTTPS://WOMENINTECHWORLDSERIES.COM/2019/07/09/SHE-CEO-MARILYN-TYFTING-CIO-AND-CPO-OF-TELUS-INTERNATIONAL/

RESILIENCE.ORG. (N.D.). WHAT IS RESILIENCE? RETRIEVED FROM
HTTPS://WWW.RESILIENCE.ORG/STORIES/2004-05-01/WHAT-RESILIENCE/

WORLD HEALTH ORGANIZATION. (2019). BURN-OUT AN "OCCUPATIONAL
PHENOMENON": INTERNATIONAL CLASSIFICATION OF DISEASES. RETRIEVED
FROM *HTTPS://WWW.WHO.INT/NEWS/ITEM/28-05-2019-BURN-OUT-AN-
OCCUPATIONAL-PHENOMENON-INTERNATIONAL-CLASSIFICATION-OF-DISEASES*

FORBES. (2017, SEPTEMBER 25). MELLODY HOBSON: HOW TO NEGOTIATE FOR
YOUR SALARY AND OTHER WORKPLACE ADVICE.
HTTPS://WWW.FORBES.COM/SITES/CRYSTALMARSHALLSQUARE/2017/09/25/ME
LLODY-HOBSON-HOW-TO-NEGOTIATE-FOR-YOUR-SALARY-AND-OTHER-
WORKPLACE-ADVICE/?SH=366BFC014C14

HARVARD BUSINESS REVIEW. (2017, APRIL 11). HOW WOMEN CAN NEGOTIATE
BETTER. HTTPS://HBR.ORG/2017/04/HOW-WOMEN-CAN-NEGOTIATE-BETTER

URY, W. (2021). GETTING TO YES: NEGOTIATING AGREEMENT WITHOUT GIVING IN.
PENGUIN BOOKS.

CARTER, A. (2020). ASK FOR MORE: 10 QUESTIONS TO NEGOTIATE ANYTHING.
SIMON & SCHUSTER.

GOLEMAN, D. (1995). EMOTIONAL INTELLIGENCE: WHY IT CAN MATTER MORE
THAN IQ. BANTAM BOOKS.

BRADBERRY, T., & GREAVES, J. (2009). EMOTIONAL INTELLIGENCE 2.0.
TALENTSMART.

MAYER, J. D., & SALOVEY, P. (1997). WHAT IS EMOTIONAL INTELLIGENCE? IN P.
SALOVEY & D. J. SLUYTER (EDS.), EMOTIONAL DEVELOPMENT AND EMOTIONAL
INTELLIGENCE: IMPLICATIONS FOR EDUCATORS (PP. 3-31). BASIC BOOKS.

BOYATZIS, R. E., GOLEMAN, D., & RHEE, K. S. (1999). CLUSTERING COMPETENCE IN
EMOTIONAL INTELLIGENCE: INSIGHTS FROM THE EMOTIONAL COMPETENCE
INVENTORY (ECI). IN R. BAR-ON & J. D. A. PARKER (EDS.), THE HANDBOOK OF
EMOTIONAL INTELLIGENCE: THEORY, DEVELOPMENT, ASSESSMENT, AND
APPLICATION AT HOME, SCHOOL, AND IN THE WORKPLACE (PP. 343-362). JOSSEY-
BASS.

CIARROCHI, J., CHAN, A. Y., & CAPUTI, P. (2000). A CRITICAL EVALUATION OF THE
EMOTIONAL INTELLIGENCE CONSTRUCT. PERSONALITY AND INDIVIDUAL
DIFFERENCES, 28(3), 539-561.

MAYER, J. D., ROBERTS, R. D., & BARSADE, S. G. (2008). HUMAN ABILITIES:
EMOTIONAL INTELLIGENCE. ANNUAL REVIEW OF PSYCHOLOGY, 59, 507-536.

GINNI ROMETTY: LEADING IN THE AGE OF ARTIFICIAL INTELLIGENCE. HARVARD BUSINESS REVIEW. (2018). HTTPS://HBR.ORG/2018/07/GINNI-ROMETTY-LEADING-IN-THE-AGE-OF-ARTIFICIAL-INTELLIGENCE

WALGREENS CEO ROSALIND BREWER ON LEADING WITH PURPOSE DURING A PANDEMIC. FORTUNE. (2020). HTTPS://FORTUNE.COM/2020/05/14/ROSALIND-BREWER-WALGREENS-CEO-COVID-19-PANDEMIC-PURPOSE-LEADERSHIP/

DWECK, C. S. (2006). MINDSET: THE NEW PSYCHOLOGY OF SUCCESS. RANDOM HOUSE.

CUBAN, M. (2011). HOW TO WIN AT THE SPORT OF BUSINESS: IF I CAN DO IT, YOU CAN DO IT. DIVERSION BOOKS.

LINKEDIN. (N.D.). THE ULTIMATE LIST OF HIRING STATISTICS FOR HIRING MANAGERS & RECRUITERS. RETRIEVED FROM HTTPS://BUSINESS.LINKEDIN.COM/TALENT-SOLUTIONS/RESOURCES/TALENT-ACQUISITION/HIRING-STATISTICS

PERLMUTTER, D. D. (2015). NETWORKING FOR PEOPLE WHO HATE NETWORKING: A FIELD GUIDE FOR INTROVERTS, THE OVERWHELMED, AND THE UNDERCONNECTED. NEW YORK, NY: BERRETT-KOEHLER PUBLISHERS.

SCANLAN, M. (2019). BUILDING YOUR NETWORK: A GUIDE FOR INTROVERTS. HARVARD BUSINESS REVIEW. RETRIEVED FROM HTTPS://HBR.ORG/2019/06/BUILDING-YOUR-NETWORK-A-GUIDE-FOR-INTROVERTS

WILLIAMS, J. (2018). WHY BUILDING A DIVERSE AND INCLUSIVE NETWORK MATTERS. FORBES. RETRIEVED FROM HTTPS://WWW.FORBES.COM/SITES/JANICEGASSAM/2018/07/19/WHY-BUILDING-A-DIVERSE-AND-INCLUSIVE-NETWORK-MATTERS/?SH=55DFE1227C14

CHIU, C. (2021). HOW TO NETWORK AS A WOMAN ENTREPRENEUR. FORBES. RETRIEVED FROM HTTPS://WWW.FORBES.COM/SITES/CHRISTINECHIU/2021/03/08/HOW-TO-NETWORK-AS-A-WOMAN-ENTREPRENEUR/?SH=18B04962687B

MENON, V. (2019). HOW TO BUILD A POWERFUL PROFESSIONAL NETWORK. BBC. RETRIEVED FROM HTTPS://WWW.BBC.COM/WORKLIFE/ARTICLE/20190212-HOW-TO-BUILD-A-POWERFUL-PROFESSIONAL-NETWORK

MURRAY, R. (2020). 5 TIPS FOR WOMEN ON HOW TO BUILD A STRONG PROFESSIONAL NETWORK. WOMEN'S BUSINESS ENTERPRISE NATIONAL COUNCIL. RETRIEVED FROM HTTPS://WWW.WBENC.ORG/BLOG-POSTS/2020/8/26/5-TIPS-FOR-WOMEN-ON-HOW-TO-BUILD-A-STRONG-PROFESSIONAL-NETWORK

NATIONAL ASSOCIATION OF WOMEN BUSINESS OWNERS. (N.D.). ABOUT US. RETRIEVED FROM HTTPS://WWW.NAWBO.ORG/ABOUT-US

NATIONAL ASSOCIATION OF FEMALE EXECUTIVES. (N.D.). ABOUT NAFE. RETRIEVED FROM HTTPS://NAFE.COM/ABOUT-NAFE

WOMEN IN BUSINESS. (N.D.). ABOUT WIB. RETRIEVED FROM HTTPS://WWW.WOMENINBUSINESSNI.COM/ABOUT-US.ASPX

FORBES. (2018, MAY 22). TORY BURCH: SURROUND YOURSELF WITH PEOPLE WHO INSPIRE YOU. RETRIEVED FROM HTTPS://WWW.FORBES.COM/SITES/MOIRAFORBES/2018/05/22/TORY-BURCH-SURROUND-YOURSELF-WITH-PEOPLE-WHO-INSPIRE-YOU/?SH=181D505A3A22

FORBES. (2016, MAY 26). SPANX FOUNDER SARA BLAKELY: EMBRACE FAILURE AND KEEP TRYING. RETRIEVED FROM HTTPS://WWW.FORBES.COM/SITES/DANSCHAWBEL/2016/05/26/SPANX-FOUNDER-SARA-BLAKELY-EMBRACE-FAILURE-AND-KEEP-TRYING/?SH=7F4D00E6274F

THRIVE GLOBAL. (2021, JANUARY 21). VIPKID FOUNDER CINDY MI: "TAKING CARE OF YOUR OWN MENTAL AND PHYSICAL HEALTH IS IMPORTANT". RETRIEVED FROM **HTTPS://THRIVEGLOBAL.COM/STORIES/VIPKID-FOUNDER-CINDY-MI-TAKING-CARE-OF-YOUR-OWN-MENTAL-AND-PHYSICAL-HEALTH-IS-IMPORTANT/**

BARRA, M. (2018, FEBRUARY 27). MARY BARRA: FROM 'IMPOSTER SYNDROME' TO RUNNING GENERAL MOTORS. FORBES. HTTPS://WWW.FORBES.COM/SITES/MARYBARRA/2018/02/27/FROM-IMPOSTER-SYNDROME-TO-RUNNING-GENERAL-MOTORS/

DWECK, C. S. (2015). CAROL DWECK REVISITS THE 'GROWTH MINDSET'. EDUCATION WEEK, 35(5), 20.

ELLIOT, A. J., & DWECK, C. S. (2005). HANDBOOK OF COMPETENCE AND MOTIVATION. GUILFORD PRESS.

KRAWCHECK, S. (2018, OCTOBER 15). HOW TO DEAL WITH IMPOSTER SYNDROME, ACCORDING TO FORMER MERRILL LYNCH EXEC SALLIE KRAWCHECK. CNBC. **HTTPS://WWW.CNBC.COM/2018/10/15/HOW-TO-DEAL-WITH-IMPOSTER-SYNDROME-ACCORDING-TO-FORMER-MERRILL-LYNCH-EXEC-SALLIE-KRAWCHECK.HTML**

BRANSON, R. (2012). LIKE A VIRGIN: SECRETS THEY WON'T TEACH YOU AT BUSINESS SCHOOL. PENGUIN UK.

SINEK, S. (2014). LEADERS EAT LAST: WHY SOME TEAMS PULL TOGETHER AND OTHERS DON'T. PENGUIN UK.

NADELLA, S. (2017). HIT REFRESH: THE QUEST TO REDISCOVER MICROSOFT'S SOUL AND IMAGINE A BETTER FUTURE FOR EVERYONE. HARPERCOLLINS.

DELOITTE. (2019). PURPOSE-DRIVEN LEADERSHIP: WHAT IT IS, WHY IT MATTERS, AND HOW IT CAN TRANSFORM YOUR ORGANIZATION. RETRIEVED FROM HTTPS://WWW2.DELOITTE.COM/US/EN/PAGES/ABOUT-DELOITTE/ARTICLES/PURPOSE-DRIVEN-LEADERSHIP.HTML

IMPERATIVE & NEW YORK UNIVERSITY. (2016). PURPOSE AT WORK. RETRIEVED FROM HTTPS://WWW.IMPERATIVE.COM/WP-CONTENT/UPLOADS/2016/03/PURPOSE-WORK-RESEARCH-REPORT-2016.PDF

AMABILE, T. M. (1988). A MODEL OF CREATIVITY AND INNOVATION IN ORGANIZATIONS. RESEARCH IN ORGANIZATIONAL BEHAVIOR, 10, 123-167.

HENNESSEY, B. A., & AMABILE, T. M. (2010). CREATIVITY. ANNUAL REVIEW OF PSYCHOLOGY, 61, 569-598.

MARTIN, R. L. (2013). THE INNOVATION CATALYSTS. HARVARD BUSINESS REVIEW, 91(6), 78-84.

WEST, M. A., & FARR, J. L. (1990). INNOVATION AND CREATIVITY AT WORK: PSYCHOLOGICAL AND ORGANIZATIONAL STRATEGIES. WILEY.

WOODMAN, R. W., SAWYER, J. E., & GRIFFIN, R. W. (1993). TOWARD A THEORY OF ORGANIZATIONAL CREATIVITY. ACADEMY OF MANAGEMENT REVIEW, 18(2), 293-321.

ANDERSON, P., & JOHNSON, L. (1997). SYSTEMS THINKING BASICS: FROM CONCEPTS TO CAUSAL LOOPS. PEGASUS COMMUNICATIONS.

CHRISTENSEN, C. M. (1997). THE INNOVATOR'S DILEMMA: WHEN NEW TECHNOLOGIES CAUSE GREAT FIRMS TO FAIL. HARVARD BUSINESS REVIEW PRESS.

COLLINS, J. (2001). GOOD TO GREAT: WHY SOME COMPANIES MAKE THE LEAP AND OTHERS DON'T. HARPERBUSINESS.

KOTTER, J. P. (1996). LEADING CHANGE. HARVARD BUSINESS REVIEW PRESS.

MARTIN, R. (2007). THE OPPOSABLE MIND: HOW SUCCESSFUL LEADERS WIN THROUGH INTEGRATIVE THINKING. HARVARD BUSINESS REVIEW PRESS.

TUSHMAN, M. L., & O'REILLY, C. A. (1997). WINNING THROUGH INNOVATION: A PRACTICAL GUIDE TO LEADING ORGANIZATIONAL CHANGE AND RENEWAL. HARVARD BUSINESS PRESS.

www.ingramcontent.com/pod-product-compliance
Lightning Source LLC
Chambersburg PA
CBHW070351220526
45467CB00001B/330